Working with People

by John L. Beckley

Published by The Economics Press, Inc.
12 Daniel Road, Fairfield, N.J. 07006

Additional copies are available from The Economics Press, Inc., 12 Daniel Road, Fairfield, New Jersey 07006. Or call toll free: 1-800-526-2554 (in N.J., 1-800-526-1128).

ISBN 0-910187-03-7
Printed in the United States of America

Table of Contents

Why This Book?

As you pick up this book, you probably have at least two questions in mind. One is what does this fellow actually know about working with people? The second is what's in it for me? Why should I bother to read it?

As far as academic qualifications are concerned, the answer is: "Very close to zero." I did major in psychology in college, and later received a master's degree in business administration from Harvard Business School. In neither case, however, did anyone say much about the science or art of dealing with people.

I remember, however, a theory mentioned by my favorite psychology professor that special ability is often the result of overcoming handicaps. A person struggles so determinedly to overcome a deficiency that he or she develops an unusual talent. Perhaps that's what happened to me in the field of working with people. I know, at least, that I started way down on the totem pole, with no talent whatsoever. Eventually I wound up building and running a successful publishing business where the atmosphere is relaxed and most employees seem to enjoy working. I like to think I learned something about working with people during the process.

Certainly, in high school and college, I didn't win any popularity contests. I was a product of the middle-class work ethic, brought up with my nose close to the grindstone, and my eyes on the stars. Those two positions may seem hard to assume simultaneously, but, in theory at least, it can be done.

My parents left no doubt that I was supposed to try hard, develop my abilities, and achieve something worthwhile. So I tried my best. I became a good student, was elected to Phi Beta Kappa, and thoroughly enjoyed myself winning eight major letters in athletics. But I concentrated so totally on my own interests, and developing my own abilities, that I barely noticed whether anyone else was alive. My college classmates rewarded me by voting me the most conceited man in the class.

Well—so be it. I've always suspected, though, that they made a slight error. If they had called me "egocentric" instead of conceited, I would agree instantly. At that time the world began and ended with me and my personal interests. I don't recall, however, having an exaggerated idea of my abilities. If anything, I underestimated them. That's what made me work so hard to improve.

About one thing, however, there is little question. As far as the ability to deal tactfully and persuasively with other people is concerned, I started out pretty close to zero. There wasn't much change in that situation until, close to the age of thirty, I became the executive officer, then the skipper, of a PT boat in World War II. Living with a crew of fourteen men on an 80 ft. boat, I HAD to learn how to deal with people effectively. So I applied myself, used all the brains I could muster, and I DID learn. The crew gradually warmed up, most of them learned to like me, and we eventually had excellent morale.

I learned about handling people not only from my personal mistakes in handling my own crew, but also from the mistakes my superiors made in dealing with me. I was late getting into the war. Having a wife and two small children, I didn't feel free to volunteer until the draft board was finally hot on my trail. Then I accepted a commission as an Ensign, the lowest officer rank in the Navy.

When I finished officer's training and was assigned to a PT boat squadron, I was one of its oldest officers. Also one of the lowest ranked—and all authority in our squadron was assigned strictly on the basis of date of rank, not ability.

My superiors were mostly college age or young twenties. They had all been in the Navy longer than I. Some of them had already been out to the Pacific once and lived through it. But not necessarily because of personal skill or ability. Now, in a new squadron, these young tycoons were running the show.

Some of these young fellows did an excellent job, more than we had any right to expect under the circumstances. Others, as might be suspected, left a tremendous amount to be desired. In some cases, the authority went straight to their heads. Others simply had no idea how to handle it. They had never held a position of authority and responsibility in business or anywhere else.

It was a frustrating situation, but I learned what I could—especially to keep my mouth shut. What else could one do? Fortunately, in two more years the war was over.

When I came home, the mistakes so commonly made in handling people were fresh in my mind. This country seemed to be suffering from endless industrial strife and bickering. Much of the difficulty, I was convinced, stemmed from the fact that a great many supervisory personnel simply didn't know how to handle people. They were constantly rubbing employees the wrong way, often for no good reason.

So—despite the fact that I was not an international expert, and despite my lack of academic qualifications —I decided to write a book. First I wrote down all the ideas I could think of from my own experience. Then I read all the books I could lay my hands on, by Dale Carnegie and others, about dealing tactfully and effectively with other people. If they had ideas that stood up to the test of my own experience and common sense, I added them to the list.

In order to make this material more interesting and intelligible to foremen and supervisors, I boiled it down and added pictures. Every page had only one, two, or three sentences of text and an amusing cartoon to illustrate the idea. It was a novel approach and I plodded the streets looking for a publisher. The fourth publisher I submitted it to bought the idea and we brought it out under the title "Let's Be Human". Surprisingly, in addition to being bought for foremen and supervisors, it became a selection of The Executive Book Club.

So why, 35 years later, bother to write another book about dealing with people? Because, in those intervening years, I happen to have started and developed a modest sized publishing business. In the process I've learned considerably more about working with people and have more practical, on-the-job experience to back it up. Furthermore, the subject is still vital and still generally underrated by business and professional schools.

I served recently on a committee of business executives who were asked to consult and advise with a state university that was reshaping its business curriculum. Several of the executives were presidents of companies listed on the New York Stock Exchange; a number of others owned businesses of their own.

The group agreed, almost unanimously, that the two most important factors in business success were the ability to deal with people, and the ability to communicate ideas. Neither subject is handled effectively in most business curricula. Somehow, the business professors seem to think that students should have learned how to communicate in their college English courses. But they haven't. College English courses try to make students "literary"; they don't emphasize practical communications. As for human relations, the subject isn't theoretical enough to appeal to many college professors. It seems too practical, too elementary. Yet the lack of this skill, elementary as it may seem, is the reason why many people fail to achieve their full potential in business.

The need for practical ideas on how to work with people is still very much alive. I also feel there's a special need for this material in book form, a small volume an executive can pick up when he has a few minutes to spare and consider an idea or two.

There's no organization to the book, so don't puzzle yourself about it. It's just one idea after another about dealing with people. Each item stands on its own feet. You can start where you want to, quit wherever you want to, and pick it up again later. No problems about losing the sequence of thought.

If you feel like reading the book from beginning to end, go ahead. But remember, the key to dealing successfully with other people lies not in what you KNOW, but what you DO. You may not find a single new idea in this whole book. But you will find ideas we all need to be reminded of and think about. Only practice makes perfect.

Give Personal Attention

Nobody likes to be ignored. One of the most important things you can do as a boss is to pay some personal attention to the people who work for you.

Some of the people under your supervision may not interest you. They may seem pretty routine . . . sort of dull. Nevertheless, you should take an interest in them anyway. Why? Because, if you don't, they won't take as much interest in their work or produce nearly as well. They will also think you are an unconcerned, self-centered individual. That doesn't make for a good work relationship either.

There is no such thing as THE world. There are billions of worlds, as many different worlds as there are people. Each of us is the center of a world of his own. Until you have shown some interest in personal worlds your employees live in, how can you expect them to be really interested in your world?

Yes, of course, they don't want to be fired. And some of them are very much concerned about getting ahead. So they will naturally pay more attention to you than you to them. But is that all you want? I'm afraid that in many industries and companies, that's what we've settled for. We've relied mainly on the big stick, not on friendship, persuasion, and inspiration. When it comes to praising people, making them feel appreciated and important, most of us have been under-achievers.

People need personal attention the way machinery needs oil and grease. They do a lot better work when they get it. Some people are so self-centered they need attention in order to function. If they don't get it for doing good work, they'll get it some other way.

How can you provide the attention people need in order to feel better and work better?

By noticing the work they do and complimenting them on good work or any sign of improvement.

By noticing work that really isn't up to their proper standard and asking about it—to see if there is any-thing you can do to help correct the situation.

By chatting with them occasionally, and taking an interest in the world they live in, the world of which THEY are the center.

By appreciating how important it is that their jobs be done well, and pointing out to them how important they are to the company.

By occasionally giving them some special task or responsibility, something that makes them feel recognized.

By asking their opinions about work problems they are familiar with, and giving them a chance to express their ideas.

By listening when they bring up a personal problem, even when you can't do anything to help solve it. Pretended sympathy may be cheap, but genuine sympathy is always appreciated.

Keep in touch with the people who work for you—close touch—and never let a good thought die. When you think something pleasant or favorable about anyone, make a note of it immediately and be SURE to tell them. Nobody, but nobody, gets too many compliments or too much appreciation. Most people get far too little. They'd be a lot happier, and do better work, if they got more.

Morale

Anybody who wants good morale among his or her employees should pay special attention to three things:

1. Keep them well informed about everything.

2. Listen carefully and patiently when they make suggestions. Encourage them to do so.

3. Show them you consider their interests and welfare.

There is too much secrecy in most business organizations. Why? Not because there is any need for secrecy on most subjects. It simply reflects the traditional (and outmoded) view that consideration of certain problems should be restricted to management only. People who are in on these deliberations consider that fact a badge of superiority.

But what, really, has to be kept secret? Only a very few things that might hurt if they were leaked to a competitor. Everything else about the company, the more people who know it the better. The knowledge will generate more employee understanding and fewer wild rumors than speculation and guesswork.

Managers, supervisors, and foremen should be encouraged to listen to employees carefully. That means concentrating on what the employee is saying, how he or she feels about it, and what he may also feel but isn't saying. Good listening means not talking back, not even thinking about your answer or comment until the employee has finished and you are sure you understand his thoughts and feelings—and you're sure he knows you do. Then think about your answer and give it.

The trouble with most of us is that we begin thinking about our response before the other person has even finished talking. And once we begin thinking about what we are going to say in reply, that's all we think about. As a result, we miss important parts of the message. We also convince the other person we aren't really listening. That's not good human relations—not good leadership. Listen first—exclusively and thoroughly. Then think and reply.

When employees take the trouble to make suggestions, it shows that they're interested. And that's what you want, even if most of their suggestions are of no value. It's a good idea, therefore, to caution managers at various levels not to turn down ALL the suggestions any employee makes. Refer one of them up the ladder every now and then, and let it be turned down, if necessary, upstairs. Otherwise employees sometimes get the idea that the boss is blocking them.

And that may well be the case. There are bosses in many areas of many companies who like to be considered the sole source of any worthwhile thinking in their bailiwick. That's one reason why so many companies that run suggestion systems have suggestions submitted directly to a committee, not routed through the suggestion maker's boss.

Some employees shun suggestion systems because they dread having to write their ideas down. An effective way to get over this hurdle is through so-called "Quality Circle" discussions where employees have a chance to bring up any suggestions and ideas they feel like. And there's no question about it: the effort pays. If management wants to open its mind, there are ideas out there that are worth money. The fact that they are proposed by ordinary, run-of-the-mill employees doesn't make them one cent less valuable.

When employees' questions are answered, their suggestions listened to, and their interests considered, the door is wide open for good morale and teamwork. If they don't appear, take another look. It probably means you aren't doing these things nearly as well as you think you are.

Give People Enough to Do

Executives frequently find themselves torn between two opposing objectives. One is to be sure to have enough staff on hand to handle the job promptly and well. The other is to keep down expenses. The purpose of a business is not merely to deliver a product or service that keeps the customer happy, but to do so at a profit.

In seeking the proper balance, however, there's another factor to be borne in mind: Easy jobs don't make people happy. The employee with much time on his or her hands is rarely satisfied. Unfortunately, there is a lot of truth in the old saying: the devil finds work for idle hands to do.

A lot of people may not have matured enough to realize it, but an easy job, one with not enough demands to fill the time, is not the high road to happiness. People get bored, and boredom breeds dissatisfaction. Departments where the work load has slacked off, where people really don't have enough to do, are almost always more rife with griping and discontent than busier, more productive areas.

With the shorter hours people work in this modern age, few jobs are really a physical or mental strain. And the worker who is really busy knows he or she is making a vital contribution. He's secure—he knows he's needed. The amount of work he is turning out day by day gives him something to be proud of rather than secretly ashamed of.

Most workers not only feel better when they have plenty to do—they work better too. A slow pace breeds carelessness and bad work habits, things that may be costly and hard to correct when the load increases.

When you are staffing an operation, it's usually better to understaff rather than overstaff. Make sure people have enough to do from the very beginning. Think in terms of a staff that will have to stretch itself —probably with overtime—to handle peak loads. Don't think in terms of a staff big enough to meet peak requirements easily, then sit on its hands for the rest of the time. That isn't a healthy situation. When things get too easy—when there's no challenge—morale is bound to drop. It's better to be shorthanded occasionally, with people going all out, than to be constantly overstaffed.

Keeping a group of people continuously occupied isn't easy, but that's the goal. Ups and downs in business, especially seasonal swings, may make it difficult. Nevertheless, good managers can do a lot to balance the activity.

The work must be organized properly, not only who does what, but when. Each person should have enough to keep him busy. And when a number of people don't, that's when the special projects should be brought out, jobs that are purposely planned to take advantage of any slack in the normal load.

A foresighted boss tries to keep a stack of projects handy—some of which might not be possible or worthwhile if the company were busy. Nevertheless they are well worth doing when people are available. And they are far better than letting people do nothing.

You never do people a kindness by making their jobs too easy. All you do is undermine their feeling of satisfaction and accomplishment. A lot of people may think they like easy jobs but they really don't. If you want happy, well-satisfied employees, the first step is to keep them busy.

Use a Positive Approach

A pleasant, cheerful smile, and a respectful attitude are two of the most effective management tools ever invented. Anyone who tries to deal with employees without using them is unbelievably shortsighted.

In dealing with customers, everybody knows you should smile and be polite. If an important customer came to visit you, you'd greet him or her enthusiastically with a big, warm smile that showed how much you liked him. You'd take his coat, give him a comfortable chair, and listen intently to whatever he had to say.

Are you always as warm, respectful, and attentive when employees come to see you, or you drop by to see them? Your relations with that employee will be much more effective if you are. Just because they're down the line a bit in prestige and authority doesn't rob them of the right to friendliness and respect, does it? It shouldn't—not if you are trying to develop an organization with strong morale and effective teamwork.

Bosses are not supposed to be figures on pedestals that people look up at, salute, and revere. A boss is supposed to be a friendly, smiling person who likes people. That doesn't mean he's a pushover. But, basically, every boss will be a better boss if he or she is also a friendly person and makes a point of showing it. This happens to be true, especially true, right up to the top of an organization.

Many of us are, by training, polite and respectful to strangers. But when we get used to having people around, and seeing them every day, we tend to ignore them somewhat. So, don't be grouchy and preoccupied. Smile at people and say hello when you pass them. Make the effort to learn more names, especially those of people with whom you have occasional contact.

No matter what your position, don't walk up and interrupt two people who are talking by starting to talk to one of them. If you're in a great hurry, and it's very important, apologize for interrupting and ask their permission to break in for a minute.

When you stop to speak to someone in a group, introduce anyone who is with you. Never treat anyone as being so unimportant his or her identity doesn't matter. If you can't remember someone's name, that's tough. But don't let that stop you from smiling and being friendly. Everybody forgets names now and then.

Don't make changes in the way people work without discussing it with them first. Even if they have to do it anyway, talk with them. Have the decency to show your concern, and your hope that it will be satisfactory to them. Don't just make changes as if it didn't make any difference whether the people involved liked it or not.

Try to run your organization in a way that treats everyone as a first-rate, respected individual. Some may have tougher jobs and higher paid jobs than others, but all of them should be first-rate individuals in your eyes. They deserve to be treated that way.

Cheerfulness, courtesy, respect—if you live up to standard in these three respects there's not too much else to worry about. The rest comes easy. The people you deal with will be on your side from the very beginning.

Soft-Pedal Disagreements

Unless you are a complete dictator—or you happen to work for one—you'll find many occasions in business when people of different views have to sit down together, work out their differences, and agree on a course of action. It's a situation where overgrown egos can cause a lot of needless trouble. It's also a place where good team players show their worth.

When you approach a situation like this, remember: the objective is to reach a workable solution and make everyone feel as good about it as possible. It is not to present YOUR ideas as the best possible answer and ram them down everyone's throat.

Don't be in a hurry to present your views. Let others speak first if they would like. Listen carefully. If you don't approve of an idea someone presents, don't boldly announce that fact. Why make enemies if you don't have to? If no one else backs up the suggested answer, it may die a natural death without the need for hurting anyone's feelings by opposing it.

If someone else's suggestions contain some good points, praise them. If they are very close to what you yourself would recommend, ask some questions. See how he or she would feel about some minor changes that would bring them in line with your ideas. Keep seeking cooperation, not a pitched battle.

If there's no choice, if you have to oppose someone's ideas, at least do it as tactfully as possible. Don't just say the ideas don't make sense and won't work. Ask questions instead. Ask proponents of the ideas what they would do in this case or that case. Ask questions that may lead the proponents themselves to face the weakness of their plan.

The object is not to embarrass participants in the conference and make you look smarter than they are. The object is to recognize and agree on the best solution with the least hurt feelings possible. When you disagree with people, perhaps the most tactful way to do so is NOT to try to convince them they are wrong. Instead, try to convince YOURSELF they are right. Then show why you can't agree—even though you'd like to. The reasons just aren't convincing enough. Besides, there is other evidence to the contrary that you can't bring yourself to ignore.

Getting along smoothly with others is part of the art business executives have to learn. Sometimes they don't, much to their own detriment.

I'll always remember three brothers I knew years ago who ran a very successful business. Each of them was a vigorous person with strong opinions. One day a friend asked the oldest one how they had managed to work together so many years without exploding.

He explained that they used to argue but found it so painfully distracting that they developed a special system for avoiding it. Whenever one of them had an idea he wanted to present to the other two, they would always listen carefully. If one of the other two agreed with him, he would speak up. If neither of them agreed, they simply said nothing. Two out of three was a majority, and any idea that didn't have a majority wasn't discussed. It was simply dropped.

Maybe, acting in this manner, they did lose a few good ideas that were proposed by one of their members and got no support. But that's life. In most cases, though, dropping the subject helped them reach the same conclusion they would have been forced to if they had wasted all day arguing. And without the personal bad feeling that might follow a fruitless argument.

Setting an Example

Did you ever see a construction gang working like crazy while the supervisor had a few beers at a nearby pub? Or slept in the shade in his car?

You probably never will. One of the most important things a boss must do, at any level, is set a good example. He is, whether he realizes it or not, the pacemaker. If he expects others to really put out, to pay attention to business and work hard and smart, that's exactly what he must do himself. There's something about human nature that makes us resent people on a higher level taking it easy while they expect us to break our backs.

This, let's face it, is perhaps the most common misconception in the business world—that people on higher levels don't have to work as hard. In most cases the reverse is true, but people on lower echelons have no way of knowing it. That's why every group, at every corporate level, benefits from having a boss who is a pacemaker, who accepts responsibility for doing not only his or her share but a little bit more. This kind of person sets an example for associates and subordinates.

Every operation works better if it has a boss who is on hand and available. One of the important things in managing a company, or any part of it, is to see that this is the case. If a group of employees start the job promptly at 8:30, things work best if their boss is also on hand at that hour—or before. If they work till 4:30, their boss should normally be there till 4:30 or later. Not that people need to be pushed all day. But if they have to work early and late, the burden is a lot easier to carry if they know their managers are working early and late too.

If there is any part of the operation you're responsible for that you can't cover adequately—you're spread out too thin—don't ignore that situation. Figure out the best boss, the best pacemaker, for that area and make him or her your assistant. Don't let performance deteriorate because you can't give it your personal attention. Supervisors and executives who can't pay personal attention to certain areas will rarely find that any production miracles have occurred while their backs were turned.

Being a boss would be a cinch if all you had to do was tell people what to do. But it doesn't work that way. You've also got to show them, show them you mean it, and demonstrate that you are not asking them to work any harder than you gladly work yourself. Bosses are in the same bind as a military leader. They can't stay in the rear ranks and shout: "Charge!". They've got to get out in front and set a good example.

Telling people simply isn't enough. If you want people to be on time, the way to show you think it's important is by being on time yourself. If you want people to be careful in observing safety rules, pay attention and be careful yourself. If you want neatness, be neat. If you want a fair day's work for a fair day's pay, give a fair day's work—and a little extra.

Bosses who make out the best in the long run are those who believe that what's sauce for the goose is sauce for the gander. They are willing to put just as much into a job as they ask of anyone else. And they do it first. They are honest-to-goodness pacesetters. They don't push people to do things: they lead the way.

The higher levels of business organizations are not a place where people can taper off and loaf, not without hurting their organization. When that day comes, it's time to retire with honor and let someone else carry the ball and set the pace.

Use Power Discreetly

Theoretically, in the United States, all men are created equal. Obviously, they don't stay that way. Some move on to greater power and responsibility. Others have to settle for less.

In order to produce goods more efficiently, and provide a better living for everyone, we join together in groups. Relatively few of us work as individuals anymore. Undoubtedly we live better as a result, but it does have one unfortunate drawback. Somebody has to be the boss. Somebody has to have the authority to decide what the group shall do and the power to back up his or her decisions. Otherwise the operation winds up in fruitless bickering and discord.

But the plain fact is that nobody likes to be bossed. Yes, we must have bosses, people with power and authority to settle disputes and keep operations on course. But the less obviously and blatantly this power has to be used, the pleasanter it is for the people involved, and the more willingly they contribute their efforts. Leadership—the ability to keep people moving in the right direction by example, persuasion, and guidance—is even more important than authority. FORCING people to do things is costly and unpleasant.

There are more than a few big egos in this world, people who obviously enjoy the fact that they have more power and authority than others. They show, in the way that they give orders and directions, that they think they are superior to the people they are in charge of. They get a kick out of displaying this superiority.

Can you blame anyone who resents this sort of bossiness? A certain amount of direction is necessary to make things work. But the person who lets power go to his head and displays or uses it unnecessarily is a fool. And everyone but he knows it.

This doesn't mean a boss should never use his or her authority to order people to do things. But it really shouldn't be necessary to ORDER people you work with every day. It should be enough to tell them what you would like them to do and discuss it if they have any questions. In most cases they will be perfectly willing to cooperate. So why bother to use a forceful, ostentatious approach? Why ORDER them to do things when they will actually perform better if you simply ask for their cooperation?

The fact that you have a boss can be painless or painful depending on how he or she develops the relationship. If you are treated as a cooperative person, who is counted on to help, that's fine. But if the boss treats you as someone or something he or she uses to carry out his or her orders, that's a pain.

How do you suppose people feel about working for you? Have you given it much thought?

Supervisors, executives, company presidents, provide the direction and control we absolutely must have to run our enterprises intelligently. But when they let this power go to their heads, if they think it makes them a little better—or a lot better—than the rest of us, that's a totally unnecessary evil. The only people who are really qualified to use power over others are those who sincerely respect the rights and worth of every individual.

A good boss treats everyone as his or her equal as a person. He never forces people to swallow their pride or self-esteem in order to work for him. He uses authority sparingly, and never interferes with the independence and freedom of the people who work for him except as absolutely necessary. No boss is as successful as he should be, or could be, until he attains these goals.

Don't Hide from Your Problems

When you become aware that one of your employees has a problem, or is dissatisfied about something, don't duck it. Face up to the situation promptly.

Tell the person that you've learned he or she is unhappy about a situation. Ask them what's causing the problem. Tell them you'd be glad to help straighten it out if you can.

If you duck a problem, it's apt to get worse rather than better. People brood on a situation. Sometimes their facts are wrong or they imagine the worst. Instead of letting them get worked up and stay that way, it's smarter to face the problem immediately, find out how serious it really is, and determine whether anything can be done about it.

At the least, having investigated, you'll know what the facts are and whether the persons who are upset really have a legitimate complaint. If they have, you should know about it. And even if they haven't, they will at least have had a chance to express themselves and get it off their chests. Maybe all you can give them is a little sympathy. But if that's the case, isn't it best that they know it now rather than later? If they can see you've considered the problem fairly, and that's all you can do, maybe they'll decide to let the matter drop.

On the other hand, if you don't take a look at the situation, their only choice is to keep on making as much fuss as possible until you do. That's why problems should be faced promptly. If you don't, they keep on festering, often unnecessarily and to no one's benefit.

Sometimes people are dissatisfied about a situation because they don't have the facts straight—it's all a misunderstanding. But until you face up to the situation and make it clear to them, they will continue to complain—perhaps under their breath, but that isn't helpful, either.

A person who acts as boss is supposed to be a problem solver, and a settler of differences. Nothing makes people respect you more than showing your willingness to do it, as fairly and squarely as possible. A tendency to avoid this responsibility leads people to suspect you are "chicken". In case there's any doubt in your mind, that isn't good.

Let's suppose, for example, that a certain branch of your business didn't get as big a Christmas bonus this year as the other branches. Actually, they didn't have nearly as profitable a year. And the company policy is to pay bigger bonuses to those branches that make the most money. But you hear there's been a lot of grumbling.

So what do you do? Instead of assuming it will pass over, you go directly to them and tell them what the policy is. "The Christmas bonus is an extra we pay when we have had a very profitable year. The branches who have made bigger profits get the bigger bonuses. When your branch makes a bigger profit, you'll get a bigger bonus." This may not stop all the complaints, but at least the facts will be on the table. There will no longer be any question as to why you did it, what you had in mind, or whether you intend to stick by your decision.

Whenever you hear of grievances or dissatisfaction, try to get to the bottom of the matter as fast as you can. When you track down gripes you will discover that many of them are due to lack of communication or misinformation. People are disturbed because they don't understand the situation. You may not be able to please everybody, but at least you can correct these false impressions.

The mark of a good manager is that he or she detects problems quickly, and gets to the root of the matter promptly. A less skilled manager often ignores the same problems until they are so severe he or she is forced to act.

A stitch in time saves nine.

Do It Face-To-Face

In dealing with people who work for you always do as much as you possibly can in person. Why? Because most people prefer bosses who have the warmth and friendliness to deal with them face-to-face. It also gives them a chance to raise objections or ask questions.

How many times have you been disgusted with memos that decided issues or reported decisions which you knew didn't make sense? It's very hard to talk back to an official memo—that's one reason some bosses like to use them. But running things by memo is "chicken", a technique used by people who don't want to explain their reasons face-to-face. No memo, on any subject, can possibly be as effective as a personal encounter where people have a chance to explain their thinking, ask questions, and make suggestions.

True, if you have to provide information about a certain subject to a lot of people, the most efficient way to do it may be to put out a memo. Maybe a meeting of all the people concerned would be too big. Perhaps smaller meetings would take too much time. But before you put out a memo to any group, discuss it first with some of the members of that group. Be sure you are on target, not making obvious mistakes people will object to or misunderstand.

Day after day, some executives grind out memos and bulletins to people about matters that really ought to be handled face-to-face. Before you put a message on paper, stop and consider. Wouldn't it be more effective to discuss this in person? Then you could be sure the person you were addressing really understood exactly what you meant. Any chance of a misunderstanding could be prevented by a few pointed questions to be sure your meaning was clear.

And, isn't a personal visit from you, or conference in your office, far more inspiring or flattering than a piece of paper?

If you let memos become the glue that holds your operation together, you are losing the warmth, and inspiration of human contact. Your people are no longer a team interacting with one another. People like to interact with other people. They don't like to be pushed this way and that, without being consulted, by people who write memos, no matter who those memo-writers are.

Memos are by no means the most effective way to run a business. In most situations they should be a last resort or a final step. Wouldn't the person you're thinking of writing to be more pleased by a personal visit? And wouldn't you make your points better and understand his or her reaction more clearly? Memos can't answer questions the recipient raises; you can. Furthermore, you can see his reaction immediately for yourself, and smooth over any hurt feelings or disagreement before they become serious.

If you are writing a memo to people who work for you, you can probably say anything you want to and make it stick. But that doesn't mean it's the best way to do it. When you sense that an idea might be offensive to people, the smart thing, usually, is to tone it down. Find some other way to skin the cat that will not make people so unhappy. If you automatically write memos, however—never discuss things with people first—you seldom find out how unpopular a certain message may be until the fat is already in the fire.

If it would take too long to visit someone, why not check by phone? Let memos be a last resort—a final step, perhaps, but not your first.

Praise Publicly—Criticize Privately

Praise publicly—criticize privately. Anyone who aspires to handle people well should understand the reasons for this admonition, then monitor his or her conduct day by day until it becomes an unbreakable habit. Because it isn't easy. The natural tendency of many bosses is to praise sparingly and in private, but to criticize loudly and publicly.

Have you even been severely criticized in front of others by someone who had authority over you and you really couldn't answer back? Think back a long ways and perhaps you can remember. It's a humiliating experience.

Yes, it does make you remember for a long time what you did wrong. But it also makes you hate the person who roasted you. Bosses who use this tactic very often are not respected. They are quietly hated. If anyone gets irritated enough to answer back, the boss himself may get a tongue-lashing. And that may be the end of that person's employment. Either way, the result is totally unconstructive.

The constructive way to criticize is privately and reluctantly. Privately—so the person criticized isn't embarrassed by the fact that other people are listening while he gets a dressing down from the boss. That leaves him free to think about what the boss is saying instead of just being horribly embarrassed. Reluctantly—so he or she can see that the boss doesn't like to do this and doesn't enjoy heckling him. But it's something that's so important it has to be done, and the boss is trying to do it as constructively and helpfully as possible.

Criticizing people without hurting their goodwill and cooperative attitude is hard enough in private. In public, it's practically impossible. Public criticism burns some people so badly, it kills all creative initiative. In the future they'll do exactly what you say—whatever they can do without fear of blame—and that's it. That's why bosses who criticize sharply, severely, and publicly, rarely achieve more than grudging compliance from the people they supervise.

People aren't stupid. When you try to criticize them privately, in a way that is helpful and not embarrassing, they appreciate it. They realize you are trying to spare their feelings. Usually, they'll do their best to correct the situation.

And what if you were misinformed or jumped to the wrong conclusion? Isn't it better if someone can tell you that privately? Less embarrassing to both of you?

Praise is a horse of an entirely different color. Praise people as openly as you like. As long as it doesn't create jealousy, the more people who hear it the better. Certainly, the person being praised won't object in the least.

Praise is a wonderful tool to help people do better work. When you have to criticize someone, one of the best techniques to make that criticism palatable is to find something to praise at the same time. Make the person feel good about his good points. Then ask him or her to improve one of his few characteristics or habits that isn't so satisfactory. A little praise helps the criticism go down a lot easier.

There's too little praise in this world. I could use a lot more. You could too, couldn't you? To help remedy this shortage I try to follow a personal rule: don't let a compliment die. Whenever I think a nice thing about someone, I make a note of it. Then I either tell him or her, write a note, or call him on the phone.

Another effective way to compliment people is to compliment them to one of their friends or associates. You can bet your bottom dollar the friend will pass the remark along to the person complimented. And he or she will like it too.

Praise publicly—criticize privately. Make it a habit. Watch yourself. When you've mastered it, you'll have something that will make you a nicer, more effective person the rest of your life.

Stay Loose!

Nothing is more helpful in dealing with people than a sense of proportion. A sense of proportion and a sense of humor. If you can keep from getting uptight— from taking yourself or any situation too seriously— you'll get much better results.

Yes, some problems are serious—but there's nothing to be gained by exaggerating their importance. One way or another the sun will rise again, the world will go on. And most problems can be handled a lot better if you can keep a smile on your face. Why get so worked up that you simply make the situation worse?

Yes, your company is important, your job is important, and your problems are important. But not as important as maintaining your poise, your fairness, and your cool. If you can maintain your sense of proportion, and a sense of humor when the world seems to be falling apart, you'll be a Rock of Gibraltar to the people who work for you. They will show their appreciation in better work and greater loyalty. If all you do in crisis after crisis is add to the heat and confusion, they will soon lose respect for your abilities under pressure.

By a sense of humor we don't mean the knack of telling jokes. We mean the ability to take some setbacks and still see that the world has not come to an

44

end. If you don't take yourself too seriously, there are always things in any situation that are still amusing, that you can still smile about. If you approach the job of patching up the damage with a smile on your face, you'll get a lot of help. And it makes a lot more sense than spreading gloom, pessimism, and blame.

I guess what we're really talking about is cheerfulness. A smiling, cheerful boss invariably wins more cooperation than a grim or gloomy one. If you're the boss of anyone or anything, don't wander around with a sour look on your face. Find something to smile about—and find it often. Do YOU like to work for anyone who rarely smiles?

Get in the habit of taking yourself and your problems with a grain of salt. Learn to smile at yourself and the world as well. Why? Because you'll get better results if you do.

It may seem silly to go around sharing smiles with people. But it isn't. It makes them feel better, and it will make you feel better too. It shows your goodwill and good sense. Against the background of time and eternity, how serious are the problems we get worked up about anyway?

No matter who's the boss and who is the worker, no matter who's on top and who's on the bottom, we're all in this thing together. We're all sharing this life—grains of sand passing through the hourglass of time. Why shouldn't we be as relaxed and pleasant about it as possible? It doesn't make sense to be anything else. Why compound our miseries by getting or giving ulcers?

If you're interested in better productivity, keep a sense of proportion and develop a sense of humor. People always do more for a boss with a lighthearted approach, and do it more willingly.

When you have serious, vexing problems, let them sit a bit until you can see them in proper perspective. Wait till you can smile at yourself and your grim situation. Then move into action, and take your team with you.

Seek Advice

When you are working on a problem, trying to make an important decision, do you ask your assistants what they think you ought to do? And listen carefully?

Do you also consult the people most closely involved in the situation, regardless of their level of authority, and see what they think?

There are a number of reasons why this is an excellent way to operate.

In the first place, it's the best way to be sure you don't miss any good ideas. Good ideas, excellent solutions, may come from anywhere. If you don't ask and invite people to make suggestions, they may not have the courage to do so.

Most people are glad to be asked what they think. It makes them feel like a significant part of the operation. They are considered members of the team. How do you feel when someone in higher authority asks your advice? Maybe we should also ask: how do you feel if he or she never bothers to ask your opinion?

In most jobs, there's not much glamour in merely doing what you are told to do or expected to do day after day. People like to be asked to do a little brainwork now and then. It gives them a lot of satisfaction to feel that they have been invited to participate in the thinking and the planning even if they can't contribute much.

Consulting people also pays another big dividend. If you habitually consult people about the changes you're considering, they don't come as a surprise. When employees have had a chance to express their opinions about something, they accept the decision more readily. When they've been consulted, they feel more obligation to give the proposed solution a fair try. You may not get 100 percent cooperation from everyone, but you'll almost always get more cooperation than if you sprang the idea as a complete surprise.

Another solid reason for constantly consulting your assistants is to give them a maximum amount of training in your job. Some day, one or more of them may have to act as your replacement. They should also know enough about your job so they can fill in satisfactorily while you're on vacation.

Some executives tremble at the idea of anyone else handling THEIR JOB. Admit it or not, they like the feeling that they are indispensable. And they are very happy to keep things that way.

Failing to train associates, however, is a serious management error, one frequently made by very intelligent people. They simply haven't faced the fact that life must go on. To be eligible to move up, a capable executive should have developed capable replacements for himself. If a company is stupid enough to use these replacements to ask him to move out, that's their loss. A boss smart enough and capable enough to develop excellent replacements, will sooner or later find a company that appreciates this talent.

Often a big reason for not consulting assistants, as well as for not delegating authority, is that an executive doesn't think his or her subordinates are competent enough. He thinks no one can handle the job as well as he can. But who knows, for sure, what subordinates are capable of until they've been exposed to problems and given a chance to develop themselves?

Every once in a while, review your key employees. In a crisis, who would take over for each of them? Discuss the situation with them and be sure each of them is seriously developing subordinates.

Don't sit in your sanctum and wait for people to come to you with ideas. Go to them with questions. Seek advice every day. It's a good way to build a thinking, cooperative organization, and boost morale at the same time.

Show Confidence in People

One of the keys to getting good work and good attitudes from employees is to EXPECT good work and good attitudes. You know you are being fair and constructive in dealing with them. Show that you assume they'll be the same in dealing with you.

This doesn't mean that some people won't try to fool you and get away with poor attitudes and subpar efforts. But when it happens, never act as though you EXPECTED them to act that way. Be surprised and concerned.

Obviously, you don't really believe that every worker is going to be trustworthy, reliable, and industrious. You know very well that some will occasionally try to fool you and get away with the least effort possible. But if you acted as if that's what you expected, what incentive would they have to perform any differently?

On the other hand—as the old saying implies, if you give the dog a good name, there's at least a chance he may try to live up to it. It's very pleasant when someone acts as if you were an industrious, reliable person. It's nice to have the boss treat you that way—so nice that people are frequently tempted to try to live up to the image. As a result, they are more apt to start doing good work, and keep on doing it, than if you had approached them with the assumption that they were basically lazy and you had to watch them like a hawk.

Don't let one or two mishaps discourage you. Keep showing people you expect them to have good attitudes and know they can do good work. Don't continually expect the opposite. Show that you see the good possibilities in people and encourage them to make those possibilities become a reality.

This doesn't mean that any boss should turn his back on poor work and pretend that it doesn't exist. Bosses have to keep their eyes and ears open. But when they see something wrong, they shouldn't assume that whoever is responsible for it is dishonest, lazy or untrustworthy.

When something is wrong, the boss has to get to the root of it. He may well find that someone has been careless, lazy or inefficient. So what should he do then? A great many bosses simply give the culprit a tongue-lashing.

But is that really the best way? Wouldn't it be more effective to act surprised and disappointed that someone with much better potentialities failed to live up to them? You expected more than that from someone with their capabilities. How and why did it happen? Instead of being outraged, be disappointed and inquisitive.

The trouble with harsh criticism is that it puts you

in the position of trying to FORCE people to do good work. And that's really a very hard thing to do. You may force people to put on the appearance of doing good work, but it won't be their best. Not unless they WANT to do their best.

It's much smarter, when people fall below your expectations, to show your disappointment, and your interest in helping them do better. Usually, if you've shown confidence in people, and they haven't lived up to it, they're bound to feel some shame. Usually they'll apologize, and try to do better.

Showing confidence and trust in people is the way to best results. If there are some people with whom it just doesn't work, give some thought to replacing THEM, not changing your tactics.

Don't Go Off Half-Cocked

It can be very exasperating to be the boss. Sometimes, when things go wrong, when people seem deliberately stupid or careless, it blows your patience.

That's the best time to do nothing—or as little as you have to to meet the crisis, if there is one. Back off; slow down. Don't act—or express your feelings—until you're cool enough to consider all sides of the situation factually and sensibly—not vindictively. When you can see a course that makes sense—action that will help the situation, not just express your resentment—go ahead.

When you're angry, it's so easy to say offensive things. In criticizing errors and inadequate work, it's easy to overlook the good side of people's records, to blame them unfairly and even mutter threats of dire consequences.

The smart tactic in situations like this is to delay action. Wait, if you possibly can, until you're back in control of yourself and know you can act in a rational manner. Wait until you are once more sensitive to others' feelings as well as your own. Blow your stack privately, first, if need be, but be sure that's the way it is—strictly in private.

Never be in a hurry to blame people. While they are still upset over an error, they are in no condition to think logically and reasonably. Wait—consider it with them later, when you'll both be more reasonable, less emotional.

Furthermore, don't run any witch-hunts to find out WHO was responsible for an error or a poor result. Really, what difference does WHO make, now that the damage is done? The objective, in a reasonable business, is not to punish anyone, but to make sure the painful experience is never repeated. Investigate HOW, not WHO! Don't engage in personal recriminations about what happened. That's water over the dam. Let's just be sure everybody understands how it occurred so we can all keep it from happening again.

Threats are rarely, if ever, a good way to influence people. A threat smacks of force. Nobody likes to be threatened. Even in cases where a threat appears to have been effective, it will always be remembered and resented.

If you reach a point where you might have to fire somebody, change their job assignment, or take some other action they wouldn't like, never mention it as a threat. Explain the situation and show them why you may have to do it, even though you don't want to. If their performance doesn't improve, you'll have no choice in the matter. Admit that it's a tough situation. Sympathize with their problem. Show that you have no hard feelings and hope they won't have any either if you are forced to take action.

Watch your attitude on a daily basis. Watch out for times when you are so concerned over what people are doing wrong that you don't give them fair credit for what they've done right. Things are seldom as bad as they look—or as good as they look either. Try to stay in balance—don't swing from one extreme to the other.

It's easy for some bosses to become overly harsh when they are excited, and besieged with difficulties. That's the time when unusually good bosses keep their cool, take the trouble in stride. And get it corrected without upsetting any more people than necessary.

They don't get angry.

They don't blame anybody.

And they don't attack anybody.

They get the train back on the track with the least disturbance possible.

Don't Accept Poor Work

Good bosses don't walk around with a scowl on their faces and big sticks in their hands. On the other hand, they can't be a pushover either. The reason for bosses is to coordinate people's efforts and, in one way or another, get them to do better work than they would otherwise.

In the old days, before there were powerful unions and so many laws regulating the treatment of employees, things were different. It's harder to discipline employees today. In addition to opposition by the unions, and tight regulation by the government, there are now so many automatic benefits for unemployed and retired workers that the threat of dismissal isn't nearly as powerful a tool as it used to be. "So what?" says the older worker. "If you fire me, I can still take early retirement, and I soon get Social Security."

"And if you fire me," says the younger one, "I think I'll take a little vacation and collect some unemployment compensation."

Meanwhile, the cost of employees has continued steadily upward—salaries, wages, health insurance, Social Security, and other retirement benefits. The boss's job—to see that the company gets its money's worth—is harder than ever and there are fewer tools to do it with. Obviously—but something many people haven't appreciated yet—bosses have to be a lot smarter than they used to be.

What do you do if you finally wake up to the fact that you don't have the punitive powers bosses used to have to FORCE people to do better work? You begin to think about your persuasive powers and use them to the utmost.

How do you make people WANT to do a better job? There are hundreds of different things. Most of them revolve, however, around paying more attention to people as individuals, appreciating their importance to you and the company, treating them fairly, and helping them improve their talents and increase their responsibilities. For years, most managers turned first to the negative, easy way to FORCE people to do what they wanted them to. The positive way is harder to find—it takes more patience—but it works better when you do find it.

If you can show that you trust people, and prove to them that they can trust you, that's the first step. And if you see that they get a fair deal, why shouldn't they give you and the company a fair deal? You have every right to expect it and you should.

And what do you do when you run across someone with whom this fair-minded, considerate approach doesn't work? He or she is still trying to get away with everything he can, whenever possible.

Having given this person a fair trial, and having used every means to find the source of the trouble, you then FIRE him or her as promptly as possible.

Good human relations must always be accompanied by quiet but firm insistence on good attitudes and good work. When you don't get them, it's your job to find out why and take corrective action. If people refuse to cooperate in your effort to help them become satisfactory employees, what else can you logically do but fire them? They are reneging on their half of the deal.

Firing people is rarely pleasant, but negative attitudes and slipshod performance are poison to an organization. Getting rid of the people who refuse to correct them usually turns out to be a healthy tonic for everyone.

Do a Lot of Listening

One of the secrets of being a good boss is to do a lot of listening.

Make it convenient for people to talk with you. Invite them to drop in and get things off their chests. If they don't come in, go see them. Then listen—with interest. Remember, keeping people in the mood to do good work—and thinking straight about their problems—is what being a boss is all about.

You can't accomplish this simply by telling people what to do, or being critical. You've got to appreciate what's going on in their minds, what problems they are thinking about, and how they feel about those problems. If you think they are off target, maybe you can catch it in time and get them back on the right track.

If a subordinate still thinks he or she is right, why not discuss it, jointly, with others who are familiar with the situation? Listen—keep your mind open to all the evidence. Then make your decision.

Frequent contact with people—not just saying hello, but a detailed discussion of how things are going—is necessary to keep some employees moving. There are people who, without stimulation, will do the same job the same way forever and ever. It won't occur to them to try anything new or different. When you talk to people like this, it's important to ask them occasionally what they think about certain areas of work. Do they have any ideas how they might be changed or improved? Have they tried anything new lately?

This doesn't mean you should put the heat on every time you talk with someone. That's too pressurized. But DO let them realize that you are always interested in what they are doing and how they are doing it.

There are also some people who are completely intoxicated with new ideas. New ideas may sound great, but the trouble is they don't always work. And if they don't work, some of them may cost you a fortune.

We once had a promotional executive who had new ideas by the dozen. We made good money on some of them. The difficulty was he couldn't tell the good ideas from the bad ones. He was always positive each new idea was a winner. Many of them we had to veto because the possible cost of trying them far outweighed any prospective gains.

You may very well have some subordinates like this. Lots of creative people are good at thinking up new ideas but very poor judges of which ones will actually work. It's important to talk frequently with such people so that (1) you know what ideas they have that might be worthwhile, and (2) you can keep them from wasting time, money, and effort on the ones that aren't.

If you have to kill an idea because you firmly believe it isn't worth trying, do it. But sometimes— to keep anyone from feeling that you are personally blocking him or her—it may be a good plan to have the person present the idea to others as well. If they agree it won't work, you're off the hook. You're not blocking anyone personally. On the other hand, if they think it's a good idea, maybe you'd better restudy the situation.

It often takes a while before people who work for you feel comfortable talking with you about their problems. Often this is caused by the fact that you interrupt too much, and are too critical. But don't give up because of that. Try to do more listening. Don't be critical, or make too many comments the first time you hear about something. Think it over. Then, later, when you talk again, ask questions that will help the person recognize the problems his or her remarks have raised in your mind.

Find some way to keep discussing people's jobs, responsibilities, and ideas with them on a fairly regular basis. It's a key to managing intelligently and tactfully.

Try "Joining Them" First

There's an old saying among politicians: "If you can't lick 'em, join 'em!" It's just as true in business. There's no use fighting losing battles. There's also no use winning battles that cost more than the victory is worth.

Whenever there are differences of opinion, the experienced executive looks, not for the ideal answer, but for a solution that will be at least somewhat acceptable to both sides. In relations between people, battles that arouse the emotions are often costly. Even if you're the winner, they leave a residue of ill will that may cost you later. It's much better, in many cases, to resolve on a middle course where each side realizes they are giving up something to achieve harmony and teamwork.

In a good business, "licking them" is a last resort, something to turn to only if it is essential and all else has failed. There are occasions, of course, when you must take a stand for what you believe. But these occasions wouldn't arise so often if people were more aware of possible differences in advance and gave more thought and effort to finding some sort of acceptable compromise.

"Joining" the opposition is no disgrace; at times it may be the only intelligent thing to do. By appreciating others' hopes, fears, and analysis of a problem —which you know you don't have a chance of changing—you may preserve a spirit of cooperation instead of resentment. This will make them far more willing to switch to your point of view later, without rancor, if their solution proves faulty.

In dealing with the people who work for you, the primary emphasis should always be on "joining" them. By this we mean appreciating their point of view, their hopes and problems; trying to help them get the solutions that are in their best interests.

By the very act of "joining" them, however, you are creating an obligation for them to join you. You then have every right to expect them to appreciate YOUR hopes, fears, and problems, and to help the company achieve its objectives.

One of your main objectives, as a boss, should be to keep you, your people, and your company on the same side of the fence. The more you can join in appreciating each other's objectives and problems, the better the cooperation will be. The best solution to any conflict of interest is one that helps both sides.

This is the ideal solution, of course, and it isn't easy to find these days. In many industries and companies, the workers are on one side of the fence, management and the owners on the other. Never the twain shall meet. Where this kind of relationship has existed for years, it isn't easy to make a fresh start. But if nobody ever tries to "join" the other fellow, why should the other fellow ever try to join him?

In dealing with union organizations, there may be limits as to how far anyone can go in getting them to "join" the company and play "Give and Get" instead of "Gimme, Gimme, Gimme". On the other hand, every individual who works for you, and every individual you deal with, is open to a mutual interest approach. If you take the initiative, and try to understand and appreciate his point of view, he'll be obliged to do the same toward you. Regardless of whether you can lick 'em or not, try joining 'em first!

Cutting Down Errors

Nobody's perfect. Everybody makes mistakes now and then, whether they are in a work crew, the accounting department, or the president's office. Mistakes cost billions of dollars a year. That's why the ability to help people concentrate on cutting down errors is an important executive talent.

A great many errors are caused by incomplete or faulty instructions. The person in charge thought his or her assistant understood clearly—at least he assumed they did because they didn't act uncertain or ask any questions. But they really didn't and nobody realized it until after the damage was done.

A good basic habit for any executive is to make sure his or her instructions are clearly understood. Teach your aides and assistants to be sure they are understood too.

Usually, the failure to understand is caused by one of three things. First, you didn't explain thoroughly enough, and check to be sure you were understood correctly. Second, the person receiving the instructions thought he or she understood, but didn't. Third, the person receiving the instructions didn't quite understand but was embarrassed to admit it.

There's a simple, foolproof method for avoiding

these problems, or at least cutting them down to a very minimum. To begin with, make your instructions as simple and as explicit as possible. Always give specific examples of what you mean.

Repeat the instructions more than once. Explain what you mean in more than one way. If the subject is at all complex, give another specific example. Give the listener more than one chance to catch your meaning.

Finally, when you've finished explaining something, don't assume the person you're talking to has understood. Make him or her PROVE it. Don't just ask, "Is that clear?" That doesn't prove a thing. If you got a dollar for each person who answered "Yes" but really DIDN'T understand, you'd get rich.

To prove that the listener understands, TEST his or her understanding. Give him a case or two and ask how he would handle it. Ask specific questions, questions designed to show whether he really understands what you're driving at. Best of all, have him repeat your instructions in his own words. Not in YOUR words, but HIS words.

This may sound like a lot of work, but it really isn't. Once you get used to operating in this way, and your associates expect it, it won't slow things down at all. And it WILL start cutting down a lot of embarrassing and costly errors.

The prevention of errors takes a lot of imagination. How can people prevent errors if they don't have the foresight to imagine where they might happen? Our company had a simple, $10,000 error in its mailing operations the other day. It was something that might have happened any time, but we had never had the imagination to foresee it and take steps to prevent it. Finally it did happen. Now, $10,000 wiser, we've set up safeguards so it can't happen again.

The best time to prevent errors, is before they happen. The possibility of error is one of the things all supervisory personnel—better yet ALL personnel— should be encouraged to look for and bring to management's attention. It's an important part of good management.

As Friend To Friend

Every once in a while, in dealing with the people who report to you, a situation may arise that you're not quite sure how to handle. What should you do, A, B, or C?

In a case like this, we recommend a very simple solution. Who is your best friend? Joe? Betty? Whoever it is, think specifically of that person. How would you treat them if you had to deal with them in the same situation? What would you do? After you've figured it out, treat the employee in question in exactly the same manner. Treat him or her like a good friend with whom you have to settle a problem, and whom you're trying not to offend any more than you can possibly help.

Let's suppose your friend Joe has been late a lot lately and you've got to do something about it. Would you call him in and give him a good bawling out? Not your best friend Joe, you wouldn't. You'd call him in and ask, in a concerned and solicitous way, what was the problem. Was he having some kind of difficulty with which you could help? Did he understand the problem he was causing you by being late, and the painful problems you would have to cause him if he didn't straighten out?

No matter how much authority you have, a friendly

approach is always the best. People work better for a friendly boss. This doesn't mean you shouldn't set high standards and insist on performance. But you can still go about it in a friendly way and look for cooperation. If that fails, there's plenty of time to get tough about it later.

If you had to reprimand your best friend Betty, you wouldn't do it in front of a bunch of other employees, would you? You'd invite her instead, into the privacy of your own office and not make a big spectacle of it. The same sort of courtesy is advisable no matter whom you are criticizing.

Some executives and supervisors are so concerned about their authority they completely ignore the fact that authority produces better results if it is used in a friendly manner. A friend is someone you like and whose feelings you respect. You can be the boss and still treat people in a friendly manner. If you do, you'll usually get a lot better results. Many of the mistakes bosses make stem from the fact that they treat some people, not as friends, but as individuals they have no feelings for and don't care about.

And what if one of your subordinates makes a stupid error? Would you imply that he was utterly careless and no good? You wouldn't do that with Joe. Shocked though you might be that he could be so thoughtless, you wouldn't come right out and accuse him of being a dummy, would you? You'd ask him how it happened, give him a chance to explain, and be kind enough not to rub it in. Your other employees would appreciate the same kind of treatment—and thank you for it by better efforts in the future.

The plain fact is that you don't have to be a tough character to get good work out of ordinary people. A genuinely friendly approach, backed by firmness and authority when necessary, will almost always produce better results. There's nothing wrong with liking the people who work for you—even though you do have to lay down the law occasionally. You can be friendly toward subordinates without losing your authority. Thousands of excellent bosses prove it every day.

Keep Your Waiting Room Empty

Most of us are well aware that our time is valuable. Not all of us, however, are equally conscious that other people's time is valuable too.

Recognizing that time is money—other people's time as well as our own—is a constructive way to encourage people to use their time more wisely. When you ignore the value of others' time, can you blame them if they do the same?

For example, what do you do about the people who want to talk with you—or vice versa? We mean subordinates—people who report to you and look to you as their boss. Do you call a number of these people to your office (or have your secretary do it), then talk to them one at a time while the others wait? Yes, your time is valuable and this is one way to be sure none of it is wasted. When you're through talking with one person, the next one will be waiting.

But what about their time? If they have to wait around, cooling their heels, doing nothing while waiting to see you, it certainly doesn't make them feel that their time is very important, does it? At least, not compared to yours.

Recognizing that other people's time is valuable is a subtle way to help them realize it too. And isn't that one of the things you have to strive for if you want an efficient operation? Being concerned not to waste other people's time makes them feel important. They are needed, wanted, and part of the team. What they do with their time is important, at least in your mind. Obviously, it should be important to them too.

If you're busy when people want to see you, do you usually let them wait? It's wiser, and makes a much more positive impression, if you find out immediately what they want. Maybe it's something you can handle in a few seconds. If not, suggest that they come back later when you can see them right away. Either that or you'll drop by and see them. You don't achieve any-thing—including a better attitude—by forcing them to cool their heels for a half hour or so.

And how about the times when you are really tied up with very important matters? They are urgent, and you don't want to be disturbed by other matters if you can possibly help it. All right—think first of the people who might want to see you. Check to find out if they need your opinion or OK on anything before you become unavailable. Then delegate authority to some-one else to handle the other matters that may come up. Make it possible for life to go on as smoothly as possible even though you won't be available to make all the decisions you normally would.

Are there some matters that are so important you don't want anyone else to make the decision? Then you better change your mind about not being disturbed. Don't expect the rest of the world to come to a complete stop just because you're busy. Somebody should be delegated to decide whether it's wise to interrupt you. Otherwise you may have a lot of expensive people doing nothing, waiting for you to be available again.

Some supervisors and executives, whether they realize it or not, are definitely bottlenecks. They don't realize that their subordinates' time is valuable too. And if you don't think other people's time is worth money, why should they?

First Things First

The only reason a business exists, and the only reason it will continue to exist, is because it supplies a product or service people want and are willing to pay for. The day it doesn't attract and satisfy customers, it will close its doors. The people working there will have to find jobs elsewhere.

Obvious? Of course! But so obvious that employees manage to forget about it time and again. How many of the employees you bump into day after day are seriously concerned about pleasing the customer? Most of them are thinking of something else: how hard they've had to work lately, how much more money they think they ought to make, how boring some part of their job is, how much better someone else is treated. Oh yes! Pleasing the customer—they know that's important. But it's not what they are thinking about.

That's where a good boss enters the picture. Good bosses think about the customer and serving the customer ahead of everything. And they make a special, continuing effort to make everyone who works for them think in those terms too. They keep reminding people of the customers they are all working for, how those customers react, and the importance—number one above everything else—of keeping those customers satisfied. To the extent a boss succeeds in this effort he or she is making a major contribution to the business. He pulls people together and keeps their eye on the ball.

It seems ridiculous to have to remind people of something that is so obvious and so basic. But people get diverted. They sometimes get so involved in personal spats, squabbles, and interdepartmental friction that they forget the customer completely.

You've heard it time and again. Susie, the executive's secretary, doesn't want to help the accounting department because she thinks Sarah ought to do it. Sarah might be glad to do it but she says it's really not her job. She's afraid she's being taken advantage of.

Department A doesn't want to change its schedule to please the Sales Department by speeding up some deliveries. The deliveries will be on time in accordance with the original schedule. Why should we change our schedule?

Meanwhile, what has happened to the customers in the midst of all this? Who is thinking of them? The business was created to satisfy their needs. What has happened? Why isn't anyone thinking of them now?

This is a major reason why bosses are needed: to keep people's minds on the objective, serving the customer, not simply on their own personal concerns.

It's a major selling job, one that a good boss pays attention to day after day. As you talk with the people who work for you, be alert to the way they are thinking. When they talk strictly in terms of themselves, their jobs and their department, stop a minute and ask them who is worrying about the customer. Keep reminding people that they are all in the same boat. Nobody will get anything out of the business for very long unless somebody does a good job for the customer.

It doesn't make any difference who is right. When petty frictions interfere with company service and hurt the company's reputation, everybody suffers. Keep reminding your people that serving the customer comes first. They can settle their private differences later.

It's Worth the Effort!

All of us seem to have trouble remembering names. So why worry about it?

For one good reason—it's an excellent way to improve your results in dealing with people. People, whether they admit it or not, are proud of their names. When you remember someone's name, he or she knows you've made a special effort to remember him or her as an individual. Most people appreciate that effort. They like to be treated as individuals not as nameless faces in the crowd.

Some people claim they can't remember names. That usually isn't so. The truth is that they don't care enough to make the effort it takes. Anyone can find ways to remember a reasonable number of names. It's just a question of wanting to badly enough.

People who habitually forget other people's names haven't thought much about the importance people place on having their names remembered. They aren't sensitive enough to other people's feelings to realize that remembering names is well worth the effort. You'll be a better boss, a better salesperson, a better anything if you can call people by name, their own personal, one-of-a-kind names.

Make it a point, when you are introduced to anyone, to get their name straight, even if you have to have them repeat it. They'll be flattered by your interest. They'll appreciate the fact that you cared enough to ask.

Keep a list, or lists, of the people you deal with, even casually, in the course of your work. Refer to it every once in a while to be sure the names are fresh in your mind. Before you work with any special group, review the names and get each person clearly in mind.

To remember names, use names frequently. Don't just say "Hello" or "Hi there" as you duck past someone in the office or plant. Instead try "Hello, George", "Good morning, Mrs. Burns", "How are you today, Pete?" When you can't remember the name that goes with a familiar face, check up on yourself. Look up the name again when you get back to your desk. If you don't make an effort to do it, it will soon be obvious to that person that you don't really care.

Some people use gimmicks to help them remember names. If Mr. White has white hair or gleaming white teeth, that should be easy. If Mr. Porter has a bend to his shoulders as if he were carrying a load, that should help too. Say the name a number of times each time you have to look it up. Whatever it takes to help you remember the names of people you work with and deal with, it's well worth the effort. It shows that you care about them and their feelings.

The job never ends. All your life you'll be meeting new people and having to learn new names as well as remember old ones. It gets harder, too, when our memories get a little older. They don't seem to work as well as they used to.

But don't let yourself off the hook too easily. Are you really trying hard to remember names—as hard as you used to? Chances are you are not. Chances are you're not paying as much attention to others as you used to. And that isn't good, either.

People's names are, to them, the sweetest music this side of heaven. Play some of that beautiful music whenever you talk with them.

Stay in Touch

Do you sometimes feel you're not in as close touch with the people who work for you as you used to be?

That's not unusual; it happens to a lot of bosses. During the break-in period—their own or the employees'—they stay in close touch with what's going on and how people feel about it. Then, as time goes on, the relationship becomes more and more routine.

As people become more experienced and dependable, they require less attention day-to-day. So that's what managers tend to give them. They get so out of touch with the people they supervise that, gradually, a barrier grows up between them. They are on one side, the people who work for them are on the other.

This doesn't happen only to bosses who are unpleasant, imperious individuals. It also happens to bosses who are very nice people. Eventually they wake up to the fact that they are not in as close touch with the people who work for them as they used to be. They wonder what happened to the wonderful, close relationship they used to have.

What happened, usually, is simple, plain, lack of attention. When you were new on the job, or your assistants were, you made a special effort to get to know them. You tried to talk to them long enough every day or so to keep track of how they were feeling, what they were thinking. They appreciated this attention and interest. It developed a sense of togetherness and team play.

People are not machines; they need a lot more than oil and grease. They appreciate attention, and not only when they are breaking into a job or having problems. They like some interest and personal attention on the part of the boss day after day. And they work better and enjoy their jobs more when they get it.

Most bosses have enough problems to command their attention and use up their time. But it's a mistake to let these problems distract you from the most important job of all: keeping the people who work for you interested and inspired—in a mood to do their best. To feel this way—and keep feeling it—people need personal attention and interest from the boss yesterday, today, and tomorrow.

Paying attention to people, being interested in them and encouraging them, is not something you can do once every six months and forget about it in between. Ideally, you should find time for it every day, every week. Whenever you neglect it for any period of time, coolness and lack of personal interest is bound to appear.

People like to work for someone who cares about them—their hopes, ambitions, fears and frustrations.

They don't feel the same about working for someone who doesn't.

Whenever you suspect you are getting a little out of touch with people, do something about it. Spend some time just saying hello and giving them a chance to get things off their chests. Find out if they have had any personal problems or triumphs they'd like to tell you about. Telling the boss about something gives most people tremendous personal satisfaction.

No matter what your other problems, spend at least a little time each day treating people as human beings —friends of yours not just handy tools of production.

When employees seem a little cool toward you—not as warm and friendly as they used to be—think it over. It may not be the result of anything you've done. It may be because of what you HAVEN'T done. You haven't taken the time to be as friendly and interested in them as you used to be. And that's a mistake, no matter how your business problems have increased or how important you may have become in the organization.

Snap Decisions

A boss who is consistent—who makes the same decision today and tomorrow for the same reasons—is easier to work for than one who is constantly changing his or her mind. People learn how he thinks and how he is apt to react to various situations. They can usually guess what he wants, and what he doesn't want, without asking. When nobody knows which way the boss is going to jump, it makes life difficult.

Bosses who are inconsistent, who don't seem to follow any rules, who want one thing one day and the opposite the next, are hard to cope with. Even though they settled for one thing yesterday, that doesn't mean it will be acceptable again today. That makes people uncertain—they never can be sure of anything.

Naturally, everybody has to change his mind now and then. When you recognize you've been wrong, the smart thing is to admit it immediately. But if you take more time making decisions in the first place, if you think problems over more thoroughly to begin with, you'll make more decisions that stick. They won't have to be changed because they were good decisions to begin with. They were made for the right reasons and backed by sound logic.

Inconsistency not only creates confusion, it leads to

complaints of favoritism and discrimination. If you treat one person a certain way, then change your mind and treat the next person differently, one or the other is bound to be disgruntled.

The answer, of course, is to force yourself to take your time. Think over any problem that requires your decision. Look at it from all angles—yours, the company's, and the employees'. Don't rush the answer if there's no reason for haste.

To get answers you can live with, try a little foresight. How will this situation look tomorrow, next week, next year? Will the situation be any different? Could anything happen that would make you want to change your mind? Would you treat everybody the same way in the future?

Some people are impatient. They tend to make quick decisions just to get a problem settled, one way or another. But snap decisions don't always hold up. Pretty soon it's obvious some of them were wrong answers, not right ones.

People who make snap decisions aren't necessarily ignorant. But they have let themselves fall into some bad habits. They don't force themselves to consider problems carefully and methodically.

When you're faced with a problem, never take the first solution that comes to mind. Look at all the possible answers first. Which one is really the best?

As you judge each one, try to visualize in your mind how it would actually work. Would it solve the problem? What new problems would it raise? What might go wrong? Would it work just as well a year from now?

Is your proposed answer based on sound principles? Would you handle a similar situation the same way every time? Are you making this decision because you really think it is right, or simply because it appeals to you at the moment? The more a decision flows from principles you would apply regardless of who was involved, the more likely you will be able to live with it.

To be more consistent:

1. Don't rush decisions—look at problems from all angles.

2. Consider all possible alternatives, not just one or two.

3. Look ahead. Visualize the possible consequences, now and in the future.

4. Base your answer on sound principles you can live with, not a whim of the moment.

When Humor Isn't Funny

Humor is a valuable tool. It's also a dangerous weapon. It all depends on whether you are laughing WITH someone or AT someone. The borderline between the two is often narrow.

Being cheerful and good-natured is one of the smartest things you can do to relax the people who work with you. It makes your leadership and directions much more tolerable. But when humor consists of making fun of or ridiculing people, it's an entirely different matter.

That kind of humor isn't funny or innocent. It's cruel. Someone is being hurt so that others can laugh. Any boss with a quick sense of humor must watch his or her step carefully. If not, in responding to situations that strike him as funny, he can easily hurt someone's feelings. And that's not what bosses are for.

The boss can offend people without even realizing it. You may think you are just joshing or being funny, but the people who are the butt of a joke may not consider it as funny. Nevertheless, nobody says a word to you about it because you're the boss. They may even laugh at your smart crack because they think they have to. But they really don't like it a bit.

One of the most skillful and effective bosses I have

ever known is now president of his company. He took his first job at the age of 13, working on a New Jersey farm. He was small in stature, the son of an Italian immigrant, and a Catholic. The rest of the work crew were big guys, native American stock, and anything but Catholic. They kidded him and rode him mercilessly all summer. But he didn't quit, and he learned something he practiced the rest of his life: Don't make fun of people who work for you or with you. Be relaxed, and laugh together with them at things that are inoffensive to both of you. Beware of things that might be amusing to you but painful to them.

It's wonderful to be able to make people smile. But when the laugh is at someone else's expense, someone who obviously suffers because of your remark, it isn't humor, it's ridicule. It's cruel, like beating a dog.

There are many offices and factories, probably most of them, in which workers get a lot of fun out of ribbing one another. These situations need watching, however. People who think they are comedians sometimes keep rubbing things in until it's unbearable. Objects of the ribbing occasionally quit their jobs because of it.

When you sense that the kidding is getting merciless, and out of all proportion, don't hesitate to take the most offensive kidders aside. Ask for a little mercy. Point out what they are doing to this person— that they are hurting him as an individual and an employee. If the kidders continue their merciless approach, your whole operation might be better off if they were replaced.

As far as the kidding that goes on in an office or plant is concerned, it's wise for the boss to steer clear of it. Otherwise you may be tempted to make remarks that seem appropriate or amusing, and you will let fly without thinking. Even passing remarks by the boss can be misinterpreted and sting like a whip. In fact, the cleverer they are, the more they sting. The safest course, as the boss, is not to join in teasing anyone.

Supervisors who stoop to ridicule or sarcasm don't win friends or willing cooperation, no matter how many laughs they get in the process. To win cooperation, supervisors must have a sympathetic, understanding attitude. Nothing reveals the lack of sympathy and understanding quite as glaringly as ridicule.

Sharing Credit

All workers like to be consulted about the work they do. They have their own ideas about how it ought to be done, and how it ought to be organized. And when they have personally helped create a new method, or suggested a new idea, they are much more interested in giving it a fair try than they would be if it were just some supervisor's brainstorm.

People like a chance to say what they think. They like to get credit for having good ideas. This is a fact every boss can apply to advantage with every individual who works on his or her team. Unfortunately, some bosses are so eager for credit they can't bear to share it with anyone else. If a subordinate comes up with a good idea, all they can think of is they wish they had thought of it first. They really don't like it a bit.

What do you do, for example, when you think of a better way for one of your employees to handle part of his or her job? Most of us just call in the employee, explain the idea, and tell him to try it. That's quick and easy. But then it's your idea, not his, and he doesn't have any stake in making it work. In fact, if it does work, he may look a little bit stupid for not having thought of it himself.

What if, instead of presenting your ready-made answer, you discussed the PROBLEM with the employee first. If he doesn't come up with your answer, or a better one, ask him to give it some thought. Some time later, bring it up again and see if he has any new ideas. Ask questions, if you can, that might lead him in the direction you want him to go, but don't be obvious. Eventually, he may come up with the idea you want, or close enough to it so you can suggest your idea. But don't present it as YOUR idea. Present it as something that his suggestions or ideas brought to mind and give him credit for doing so.

If he never gets around to thinking of the idea you want, or even close to it, you may have to present it yourself. But don't do it as if you were presenting one of the great ideas of all time. Mention it casually, as if it had just occurred to you while you were talking, and see what he thinks of it. Then ask him to try it out for you and see how it works. Treat it as something that occurred to you because the two of you were discussing the problem. Get him in on it—give him credit for making you think of it.

It's a plain, easily-observed fact that people carry out their own suggestions—or suggestions they've had a part in developing—much more enthusiastically than suggestions that are thrust upon them from the outside. If you're so brilliant you never need anyone else's suggestions, don't flaunt that fact. Do your best to disguise it. It takes more than good ideas to make a top-notch organization run. It also requires cooperation and sharing the credit.

Cool It!

There are enough troubles in this world without making big troubles out of little ones. Never start with the assumption that something is a big problem. Most problems are little problems to begin with, things that could be resolved by some sympathetic attention and some common sense. What turns them into big problems is the fact that some human beings get so emotional and excitable.

When people get jumpy and irritated with one another, it's easy to turn molehills into mountains. Sometimes the cause of the trouble is an inexperienced or testy supervisor. When people don't do exactly what they were supposed to, he takes it as a personal insult. Instead of simply investigating, and giving people a chance to express any objections, he's ready to fight.

When you get a report from one of your assistants that so-and-so won't do this, or refuses to do that, how do you react? Actually, it shouldn't excite you at all. It should, however, immediately alert you to get the facts. Most problems aren't solved by issuing orders and forcing people to do things. They are solved by listening, letting people get things off their chests, then explaining what the answer has to be and why. Usually, that will settle it. If it doesn't, there's plenty of time later to be as firm as you have to be.

The best bosses rarely get excited. They keep calm, take it easy, and try to avoid forcing people to do things. They'd much rather use a little reason and common sense to convince, or at least win the reluctant cooperation, of those who disagree. They know that head-on collisions—no matter who wins—leave a bad taste in everyone's mouth.

Most employees tend to do what they are supposed to do. Sometimes they may get a little vociferous, but if you listen to them and handle them with understanding, they'll usually fall in line. All it takes to handle their usual objections or complaints is the patience to listen and explain things a little better.

When people do do something wrong, there's nothing to be gained by blowing your stack. The sensible thing is to stay relaxed, ask questions, and listen. Find out why they did it. Getting angry before you even know what caused the situation doesn't do a bit of good. It simply makes people even more uncooperative.

Sometimes people cause trouble simply because they misunderstood instructions. No use losing your cool about that. Sometimes an employee may be convinced that what he or she did was right. The constructive answer to this is to talk the situation over, listen to his views, and explain yours more fully. Once they understand you better, even if they disagree, employees will usually go along with your decision. And any kind of agreement is usually better than using dynamite.

People will sometimes deliberately do something wrong just to get your attention. They may be brooding over a grievance, or feel an urge to defy your authority. Yet all they really want is a chance to talk with you and blow off some steam. It's a little incident —why turn it into a big one by losing your temper? Give them a chance to voice their complaints and the trouble will evaporate.

Don't make an issue out of anything unless you absolutely have to. Human beings are emotional and excitable—that's par for the course. So, before you lower the boom on anyone, give him or her a chance to cool off, back down and save face. It will pay off in goodwill and good work.

Be a Builder-Upper, Not a Deflater

Most of us have an exaggerated idea of our abilities. That probably includes you and me. Not that we're conceited, but we do know our own abilities better than other people do. We also think we could do a lot better if we really tried. Therefore, in our own minds, we usually give ourselves credit for being better than we appear to be.

Furthermore, we don't like to be told that we're not really as good as we think we are. Nobody likes to be deflated. Most of us resent it deeply and remember it with bitterness.

Therefore . . . if you don't want to be disliked and resented, be careful not to deflate people. It really isn't necessary. Unfortunately, most bosses who do it cut people down in order to show how superior THEY are.

The other day, for example, I played golf in a foursome with an executive who was telling about a supervisor who works in his department. The man had come to him asking to be promoted to another job. The job was a couple of steps up. He obviously hadn't had the experience required and the job demanded abilities he had not demonstrated. The executive was so taken back by the man's nerve in asking for the job that his spontaneous answer was: "Hell, no!"

People who don't approve of profanity will disapprove of his answer for that reason. We are more concerned because it was needlessly harsh and aggravating. Furthermore, the executive followed up with an outspoken analysis of how little ability the man had shown compared with the needs of the job. There is no question—he deflated the man and put him in his place. But was it the smart thing to do?

It will take years before the employee in question will forget the harsh manner in which his request for that promotion was handled. Yet the same situation could have been handled with no abusiveness at all. The executive could have congratulated the man on his ambition, then reviewed the abilities and experience required in the job. Without saying flatly that the man didn't have these qualifications he could have, in a very friendly manner, pointed out the company hadn't seen him in this kind of situation enough to be sure he could handle it. Also that there were other people, who, in all fairness, had to be considered too.

Cutting people down is not the way to get better work. Just the opposite is true. Build people up. Encourage them to believe they are capable of doing better work—then urge them to do it. When someone has to be disappointed, don't rush up and burst their balloon. Think a bit about how they must feel. Then show that you appreciate their feelings.

People are often presumptuous in their requests

and desires—presumptuous in someone else's eyes but never their own. And they don't like it when anyone implies that they are being presumptuous—particularly the boss. Smart executives, therefore, never take it on themselves to rub anyone's nose in the painful truth. They answer unreasonable requests in a factual and sympathetic manner. There are enough things in life for people to feel resentful about without creating additional cuts and bruises that are easily avoidable.

When and How to Delegate

The most frustrating boss I ever worked for was the president of a public relations agency. He would never tell you, in so many words, what to do. But neither would he give you clear-cut authority to use your own judgment. Instead, he would just sort of sit back in his chair and wait.

If the way you handled the problem worked out all right, that was fine. It was what he expected of you. If it didn't work out, you were dead wrong. You should never have gone ahead without his approval.

To delegate or not to delegate is an eternal problem with managers. Is it better to turn a responsibility over to someone else or carry the load yourself?

Executives have assorted reasons for not delegating a responsibility to others. They may think the person is not capable enough—he might not do it well. On the other hand they may suspect that others might perform the function too well. That would make the executive seem less important, less indispensable.

A lot of business executives live out their careers cautiously, avoiding risks and holding tightly to all strings of authority. Few of this type, frankly, are outstanding. To be a really successful executive, you MUST delegate. You must continually be training the people under you and giving them more authority. That not only pleases and improves the people who work for you, it gives you time to work on new ideas, and frees you for new, bigger assignments.

Delegating authority doesn't mean abruptly turning your back on responsibility. It means training other people to handle it, giving them more and more trust to do it on their own, and checking back frequently during the early stages to be sure things are going smoothly and to praise their progress.

Employees need to be carefully trained and supervised in new assignments, but not forever. At some point they should take over full responsibility—and most of them want to. People with reasonable confidence in themselves don't want to be tied to anyone's apron strings. Unnecessary interference and excessive supervision take the joy out of working.

All workers need good clear instructions. Sometimes they may need more than that—especially if the job is new to them. But the constant goal, with all kinds of workers, is that eventually they should know the job well enough to practically supervise themselves. Once they know the job there's no need to stand around watching every move like a hawk.

Even less competent workers should be trained, as far as possible to take responsibility for their own work. You'll have to take extra pains to make them understand, and check up more frequently, especially at the beginning. But there's no reason to create or tolerate a situation where you have to stand by forever and dictate every move. People should be trained how to do their jobs right, and accept responsibility for their own performance.

Some supervisors like to have people running to them frequently for decisions and instructions. It puffs up their feeling of importance. Others are afraid to delegate responsibilities because they don't quite trust the people who work for them. They are never confident anything has been done right unless they have personally supervised every detail.

But how much can one person do or personally supervise? Bosses who make a practice of delegating responsibility, and do it intelligently, get a lot more done. They develop the capabilities of the people who work for them so they accomplish more.

Play No Favorites

It's perfectly natural to like some people better than others. They have likes and dislikes similar to your own and you enjoy their company. Other people may seem stiff or hard to warm up to.

But natural as it is to prefer some people over others, that's exactly what a good boss must strive to avoid. In business, everybody wants an even chance. If they feel you're treating someone else better than you treat them, they resent it. That's why a good boss not only has to be fair—he has to bend over backwards and be SCRUPULOUSLY fair. Whether you like some people or not, fairness demands that they all have the same chance and you measure their performance by the same standards. Those standards of measurement must be obviously impartial.

Have you ever worked somewhere where the boss obviously had his own favorites and they got preferred treatment? If you weren't one of those preferred few, it wasn't very pleasant, was it? If you really want to be fair—and to be considered fair by everyone who works for you, you must be careful to avoid letting personal likes and dislikes affect the way you treat people. Workers don't like favoritism; they tend to lose respect for a boss who doesn't treat everyone on an equal basis.

But don't bosses have the right to have favorites? Isn't that one of their privileges? Some bosses seem to act as if it were, but it isn't. When you are in a position of authority, you have an obligation to reward people in accordance with their performance. If you don't, you are undermining the morale of everyone involved.

A smart boss always takes a minute to think how this will look, not only to the person involved, but to everyone. Is this special treatment others could resent? It isn't enough to know you've been fair and impartial—hopefully it should be obvious to others too.

Use a little foresight to avoid situations that might lead to accusations of favoritism. As much as possible, pick your social friends outside your business. Either that or make a point to be equally friendly with all the people who work for you.

Watch out for people who try to "cozy up" to you and get in a position where they can ask you for special favors. Point out, in a friendly way, that your job demands that you treat everyone equally—you can't enjoy the luxury of special friends. And don't get in the position of being personally obligated to anyone who works for you. It makes a bad situation.

Sometimes one of your employees may deserve a special privilege or favor. If so, grant it openly. Let everyone know you did it and why the person deserved it. A word of explanation will help prevent misunderstandings.

And what about the dirty work? In any organization there are a certain number of unpleasant tasks. Be sure to see that these are distributed as evenly as possible. Rotate responsibilities so no one can complain that he gets ALL the dirty work. Be OBVIOUSLY fair about it. If one or two people have to bear the brunt of a hard job, be sure they understand why it has to be that way. Show that you are conscious of and appreciate their extra effort.

Being scrupulously fair is worth the time and thought it takes. You're bound to get occasional charges of favoritism anyway, but, if you've been obviously fair, such accusations will usually be recognized for what they are, unjustified complaints.

Salesmanship Is Vital

If you don't work in the sales department, you may never think of yourself as a salesperson. Yet the fact remains that every executive who works with other people—on the same level, above, or below—has to be a good salesperson. Otherwise many of his or her ideas will never find their way into action. Those that do will rarely get wholehearted, enthusiastic support.

Many of us grow up in business with the simple idea in mind that, when we achieve a certain amount of authority, all we'll have to do is tell people what to do and they'll automatically do it. Maybe some of them will. But they won't do it nearly as willingly or as well as they would if we asked them to do it pleasantly, and explained how valuable their service would be, how necessary, how helpful, and how much we would appreciate it.

No matter what their position, people are still people. They enjoy being treated with respect and consideration. And they always do a better job if they understand why it's important to you and to them. That's why successful executives are good at selling— and they always will be. Salesmanship is vital in keeping people together and working as a team.

One of the best habits you can form is—before you

ask or tell anyone to do anything—think for a moment: what's in it for him or her? Will the effort be a valuable help that you will appreciate? Then say so. Will doing a good job of it be valuable to the company? Might it even attract some favorable attention? Mention these possibilities. It makes much more sense than simply saying: "Do this" or "Do that."

This, even though you may never have realized it, is one of the vital things that distinguish the most popular, effective executives. They don't just give you a job to do. With every assignment they also try to give you a little inspiration, pointing out the importance of the task and the credit you'll get for doing it well. Or, if the assignment really isn't that important—what a relief it would be if you would handle it for them, and how much they would appreciate it.

Why waste time with this sort of approach? Because it doesn't take much time and it's definitely not a waste. It makes working for you more enjoyable and meaningful, not just an unavoidable chore.

If people WANT to do something that you ask them to do, they'll do it quicker and they'll do it better. That's why sales ability is so valuable. When you're dealing with people, don't just think of yourself as the boss who tells people what to do. Also, think of yourself as a salesperson whose job it is to interest people in constructive ideas, attitudes, and actions.

The basic job of a salesperson is to make the prospective customer WANT to buy. When you're trying to sell anything, you've got to think in terms of the other person's point of view. People can't get very enthusiastic about neatness and good housekeeping, for example, just because you want a better looking, neater department. But if you point out that neatness of the department attracts attention to them as excellent workers, that's more interesting!

A little sell is always worthwhile. Whatever it is you want people to do, think it over and figure out why it's to their advantage to do it. Better quality work, for example, means more personal satisfaction, a better reputation, and a more secure future.

Don't assume that people always know, automatically, why they should do better work. Keep reminding them, tactfully, why it pays. Keep selling. That's an important part of an executive's job. Don't neglect it.

Patience, Patience!

They say you can't teach an old dog new tricks. It isn't easy to teach people new tricks either. Managers constantly underestimate the time it will take to get workers adjusted to a new method or technique. And when employees don't catch on as quickly as you think they ought to, there's a great temptation to blow your stack. Unfortunately, that doesn't seem to help the situation.

Let's suppose, for example, that you have decided to computerize the handling of new accounts. You explain it carefully, and show employees how to do it. But some of them just can't seem to get the hang of it. It's exasperating. Meanwhile the work is getting backed up and service to customers isn't what it ought to be.

What's wrong with people? Why can't they master a new procedure? It isn't difficult; actually it's relatively simple. It's almost as if they were just being obstinate.

Well, maybe they are being at least a little bit obstinate. But nobody likes to change—to give up the habitual, comfortable way of doing things and to learn a new one. People knew the old method perfectly. Now they are nervous and keyed up for fear they'll do something wrong. Why in the world did the management have to change things?

That's why change is seldom as easy as it looks. You have to explain things, then ask questions and reexplain. And you can't be rough about it. Otherwise you'll scare people, paralyze their thought processes, and slow things down even further.

The only constructive answer is patience and more patience. Instead of lowering the boom on people, cheer them up with a smile and tell them you know they can do it.

And don't expect to get the job done in a hurry. Keep going back, checking up on people again, and helping them again. Eventually they will learn—and they'll get things right. But it will happen a lot faster, with less upset, if you realize that changing people's work habits is never easy. So don't expect it to be.

Persuading people to do better work and helping them do it is an executive's never-ending assignment. Even though a change seems relatively simple, it's rarely that easy. What's involved is breaking old habits and forming new ones.

You can't tell people something once and expect them to do it. People aren't built that way. You've got to keep telling them, over and over, and don't expect them to make the adjustment in ten seconds. The average person doesn't learn—doesn't change his or her ways—that easily.

But be stubborn as well as patient. Never give up trying to help people improve their performance. Keep plugging, and be grateful for a little progress at a time. Flying off the handle doesn't help; it just upsets people. The way to get lasting results with people is through patience and persistence—there are no miracles.

Honesty Is Basic

Perhaps we shouldn't even bother to mention honesty in this discussion. That's something you learned at your mother's knee—or across your father's lap—or you didn't. And maybe there's nothing we can do about it at this late date.

Nevertheless, we can't ignore it—the most important single factor in dealing with people is complete and utter honesty. People will put up with a lot of shortcomings in a boss, but, if he or she isn't completely honest and fair, they will eventually become well aware of that fact. It will poison their relationship.

Some folks think handling people successfully is largely a matter of being clever. But cleverness soon becomes obvious. And it's a poor substitute for sincerity and good intentions. You can't build good relations with people by trying, time after time, to use them for your own ends.

A fact we have personally observed for scores of years—and which we think no experienced manager will deny—is that those who get the most out of others give the most. A good relationship with workers and associates starts with the resolve to treat other people fairly, honestly and considerately. If you start with that in mind, there are a lot of things you can do to get better results.

If we, or anyone else, recommend a tactic for dealing with people that doesn't reflect the way you honestly feel, don't do it. Insincerity has a strong odor. Sooner or later everyone is bound to catch a whiff of it. You can't fool everybody all the time and it's ridiculous to try. People know when they are being "handled" and they don't appreciate it.

Whatever you do to influence people, do it thoroughly, honestly and completely. Don't do it just enough to make an impression then quit. If you do something insincere, the results—no matter how pleasing they may seem at the moment—won't stand up very long. And they can't make up for the loss of integrity.

In dealing with people the best policy is to avoid cleverness as you would the plague. Be completely open. Don't avoid questions, hide facts, or evade an issue by trickery. Be direct. Put the cards on the table and keep them in plain sight. Don't let anyone get the idea you are going behind his back on anything.

As a leader, the best possible impression you can give people is that you are sincere, square-shooting and aboveboard; that you are honestly trying to consider their interests as well as yours and the company's.

Some people might think we're silly—that's their privilege. But in dealing with people we think honesty is not merely the best policy—it's the only policy. It's the cornerstone on which everything else rests.

Decisions, Decisions

If you're the boss of a particular area, or of a whole company, does that mean you make all the decisions? It shouldn't. What it means is that you are RESPONSIBLE for all the decisions. If some of those decisions don't work out right, it's up to you to do something about it.

The best solution, if you can find capable assistants, is to turn part of your responsibility over to each of them. Make them responsible for run-of-the-mill, everyday decisions. If something unusual comes up, or if they are uncertain about something, you expect them to consult you.

But what about the more important decisions? Are they yours and yours alone? Yes, the responsibility is yours. But executives who hug such problems to their chests and avoid sharing them with others are short-sighted.

When a smart executive is considering an important problem, he or she usually seeks out the opinion and advice of anyone in the company, from top to bottom, who might have some insight into the situation. He talks over the situation with each of them. Finally he puts all the advice together and, using his own experience and common sense, reaches a decision. It may not be the decision he would have reached solely on his own. Chances are it's at least a little better, perhaps a lot better. At least he has made an effort to cover all the angles, not just his own viewpoint.

We have discovered in recent years that the people who work on a job are often aware of things that might be done better. Why don't they volunteer the information? Because nobody has asked, and they feel their immediate superior might resent their advice. Why haven't their superiors asked their opinion? Who knows? Conceit, ignorance, or maybe it was beneath the superior's dignity.

Quality circles, originated by the Japanese and now being adopted here, get employees together to discuss production problems. The number of valuable ideas they have brought forward are amazing.

Good executives talk to people. They sound out associates at every level to find their opinion on various problems—and also to see if they are aware of problems that they aren't. Quality circles are good—when people start thinking together they stimulate each other. But an executive who gets around and talks to people doesn't need them nearly as badly as one who doesn't.

When it comes right down to making a decision, should you always do what you think best? Yes and no. You shouldn't be pushed into making any decision you don't approve. But what if other opinions are strongly different from yours? Better take a while to think it over. If you go along with the majority opinion—especially a big majority—there will be a lot of people who agree with you, and a lot of people who feel an obligation to help make the decision work. That, in itself, is a factor to consider. But after considering this, if you still think you are right, and you think it's important enough to do it in spite of the contrary opinions, make your own decision and stick with it. After all, it IS your responsibility.

There will be a number of occasions where you disagree with a solution subordinates have recommended. At that time, think a minute. How important is this situation? If it really doesn't make too much difference either way, go with your subordinates. And tell them you are doing it even though you don't quite agree. You don't want to overrule them. This will put the monkey on their backs. It will make them want to be pretty certain their solution is likely to work. Either that or withdraw it on second thought and accept yours.

People do like to try their own ideas. They don't like to be overruled day after day about everything. So don't do it. Where possible, let them grow. Let them make the cheaper mistakes and learn from experience.

The Line Executive

A line executive's job is to help others do a better job. His greatest value to an organization lies not in what he accomplishes personally, but in increasing and improving the effectiveness of others. The work he or she does with his own hands and brain is secondary.

There are a lot of valuable employees who spend their time at their desks, reading reports, writing reports, thinking, studying records and keeping records, planning various programs and activities. But important as they may be to the success of the business, they are not line executives. They are not line executives until they get up from that desk and execute—help others do a better job, supervise their activities, praise them and encourage them, and correct their errors.

Many jobs are part supervisory, part personal work and paperwork—letters, memos, research, and record keeping. Unfortunately, the part that is most apt to be neglected is the supervisory function. If a report isn't in on time, somebody checks up on you. But if you're not supervising your people as closely as you should, it may not even be noticed. Not right away anyway.

Paperwork, reports, and records are essential. But

people who put these duties ahead of supervision are betting on the wrong horse. Personal supervision is vital to get the most out of any group. When the paperwork load becomes so heavy it interferes with active, personal supervision, it's time that some of these duties were passed on to others.

The people who work with you need your attention. They would like to be proud of themselves and their jobs. They'd like to think that they really matter—that they are needed and wanted—that they are important to someone. Nothing is more depressing than to feel like just another grain of sand on the beach.

The need for personal recognition and appreciation is something that anyone whose job is handling people—who is an executive—should take to heart and think about every day of his or her career. If you can make people feel needed, wanted, and important, if you can make them proud of themselves and their work, they'll do a terrific job for you. But you can't do this with records, memoranda, file copies, or shuffling papers at your desk. You've got to see people and talk with them—frequently.

Good supervision means being on hand—not necessarily with every person every day—but frequently enough so you understand the work they are doing, and see that important jobs are started right and progress satisfactorily. It means spotting errors and misconceptions early, before they are expensive;

detecting unsatisfactory work and methods before costly damage is done.

The trouble with most of us is that we take too much for granted. As long as people perform their jobs satisfactorily we tend to forget how important they are to us. Instead, we should be appreciating, day after day, the skill and attention it takes to do their jobs right and thanking them for it. As you watch people working, get the habit of thinking about their jobs. What does it take to do them well? Alertness? Concentration, strength, endurance, a sharp eye? Notice these things and let people know you've noticed them.

One of the greatest incentives you can give people to do good work is praise, not criticism. Praise what's good; help them correct the bad. If you make doing good work a thoroughly enjoyable experience, they'll be glad to do it again. It seems ridiculous to contend that such a little thing can make a difference in people's performance. But it can. When people from the top down make a point of encouraging good work, and appreciating and praising it, it can turn an operation around in its tracks.

The Fear of Change

People don't like to change the way they do things—
even highly intelligent people. Change is not comfortable. It makes them uncertain and uneasy. The fact
that the change seems reasonable and logical makes
little difference. It's still a change, something they are
not accustomed to. And who knows how it will work
out in the end. Why not leave well enough alone?

The important, well-educated, prestigious people
who have bitterly opposed vital changes in our life-
style are almost unbelievable. General Billy Mitchell
had to fight the entire hierarchy of the Army and
Navy—and get court-martialed in the process—before
he could convince Congress to build an air force.
Lt. William Sims, U.S. Navy, had to go around his
superiors and write directly to President Theodore
Roosevelt before he could get the Navy to adopt a
superior method of aiming its guns, a method already
proven by the British. Nurse Margaret Sanger, when
she first began to promote the idea of birth control,
had to leave this country for several years for fear
of arrest.

The same sort of opposition to change exists today.
Most people are instinctively opposed to new ideas
that might alter their lives. Yet, at the same time,
change is absolutely essential. Countries, companies,

117

and people must continue to experiment with new ideas. Those that don't find themselves falling behind.

So what do you do about it, as an executive who has to promote beneficial changes and see that new ideas get a fair test?

In the first place, don't introduce a new idea as something drastically new and radical, or as something you intend to put into effect right away. Just discuss it casually as an interesting possibility. Admit that it might not be so much of a change anyway. Emphasize the points of similarity with things you have already done successfully, or others have done. Don't push it. Just let people think about it and get some reactions.

Later, bring it up again. Mention some of the additional advantages that have occurred to you or been pointed out to you. But don't push it. Just talk about it as an interesting possibility. Listen to other opinions.

Finally, when you think people have gotten over their original fright at something new—when you've discussed it enough so the idea isn't totally strange— think about how you might introduce it. Is there any way you could break the idea down into segments and introduce it one piece at a time? A few small changes, made sequentially over a period of time, might be much less upsetting than one big one. It might not be possible, but it's worth thinking about anyway.

If the resistance to an idea is obviously too great, it may be wise to drop it for a while. But don't forget it. Bring it up again later in a form that might raise fewer objections, or at a time that might be more favorable.

Remember, logic alone will not win your case. You may be able to force a change on some people regardless, but you can't make them like it. And if they are not going to like it, better think carefully before you do it. People who become dedicated to forcing through changes they believe in, regardless of the consequences, sometimes forfeit their careers as a consequence.

Galileo was the most brilliant man of his age. With his telescope he proved the theory of Copernicus that the earth was not the center of the universe. The earth and the planets revolved around the sun. Yet, when he tried to change people's beliefs he was thrown into prison and spent the rest of his life under house arrest.

Change is essential to progress but rarely easy. Don't expect it to be.

Be Realistic

There's an old saying you may have heard from World War II: "Loose lips sink ships." It means you should keep your mouth shut about future movements if you don't want the enemy to be waiting for you with bombs and torpedoes.

A parallel saying in business could be: "Loose promises destroy morale."

It's tempting, when you are talking with people who work for you, to paint an optimistic picture of the future: pay raises, promotions, etc. It's exactly what they want to hear. It makes them feel good, and that makes you feel good too.

But what if it doesn't come true? What if things don't work out that way? Loose talk has a way of backfiring. It gets people hopped up with false hopes, then they have a bad letdown. No matter what you gain for the moment, in the long run it doesn't pay.

Employees don't forget promises the boss makes. It makes no difference whether you are obviously being grossly cheerful and optimistic or not. When you talk about their hopes, ambitions, and future, they'll remember every word you say. Not only that, but give them a little time, and they'll make your predictions even stronger. If you predicted that they MIGHT get an important promotion or raise by the end of the year, the prediction will soon be considered a definite, clear-cut promise. If you don't make good, you'll be hearing the complaint: "But you promised . . . "

This is not unusual. It happens all the time. Wishful thinking distorts the picture. Let someone brood for a couple of weeks about a casual remark, and he or she may come to regard it as a holy commitment.

Be careful! Never promise, or appear to promise, more than you know you can and will deliver. And make sure no one thinks you have promised it. Misunderstandings like this can cause a lot of disgruntlement.

The best policy, when you are talking with an employee about his or her future, is stick to the facts, even when they are not all pleasant. There's no cause to be unduly pessimistic, but do be realistic. If you paint too rosy a picture, you may be hung with it. Keep the people who work for you aware of all the possibilities, the less favorable as well as the more favorable.

There's nothing mean about acting this way. The truth is the truth, and in sharing it with them, rather than misleading them, you are being a real friend and a considerate boss.

In dealing with employees some bosses act as if everyone in their company or department had an unlimited opportunity. But unless a company is growing like a rocket taking off for outer space, that's a plain, ordinary lie. The number of better, higher paid jobs in a company doesn't always increase as fast as the abilities of the people who work there. Some people, if they want to move ahead faster, will have to quit and find a better opportunity elsewhere.

This is a fact of life—so why not face it honestly with the people who work for you? Some of them may actually decide to quit and go elsewhere. But that's as it should be. No company should try to keep people captive. Those who go will realize that you have treated them openly and honestly; so will the ones who stay. Your company will be a better place to work as a result and you'll be a better boss to work for.

Despite the fact you've heard it before, it wouldn't hurt to say it again: "Honesty is the best policy." Not merely when it seems to your advantage, but all the time.

What About the Other Fellow?

A young man who had just received an important promotion and been moved into an impressive new office invited his wife to meet him at the office, then go out to dinner. She was shown into his new office, sat down and looked at him a moment, then started to sob. "Diane, what's wrong?" he asked.

"Oh, Jeff," she said, "it's the same every time. Whenever I wear a new dress, you don't even notice."

Typical of us human beings. We're so concerned with our own achievements, possessions, and things that relate specifically to us, that we completely ignore the other fellow.

A good leader learns to conquer this tendency. He or she deliberately avoids blowing up or dwelling on his or her achievements and abilities. He takes honors and success in stride, and makes a point of praising the other fellow, not himself. Why? Because he realizes that people who may not have achieved as much progress and success as he has need the credit and praise more than he does.

It's a plain, ordinary fact, observable in almost any company, that success tends to go to some people's heads. They begin to get a little pompous and take themselves too seriously. And when they do, it's obvious to everyone.

When you win a promotion, stop and think about it a moment before you celebrate too wildly. What about the other people, the people who didn't make it? Whether you're a department head or the president of the company, there are undoubtedly others who would have liked the job, and who feel that they were just as well qualified. It's a bitter pill to them. If you make a big deal out of your advancement, it will make them feel even worse.

So don't do it. Take your successes and achievements in stride. Show that you don't regard them as absolute proof that you are one of nature's superior creatures.

Why be so modest? Why show so much consideration for people who have been, in a sense, your competitors? The first reason is simple human decency. It's a tough blow for them and the way you handle yourself is important. If you are modest and don't make a big deal out of your success, it will soften the blow. Doing so is a matter of plain ordinary kindness.

And don't forget, in the future you will want the cooperation and goodwill of these very people, not their festering, continuing resentment. Nobody likes to work for bosses who take their success too seriously, and who are forever impressed with their own importance.

It's helpful, too, if a boss stops now and then and realizes that the ability to run a business is not the only worthwhile ability in the world. Nor is it necessarily the most important. There are many intelligent, highly talented people who don't get very far in business. But that doesn't mean they are the least bit inferior, as people, to those who do. The boss who takes time to remember that and appreciate it will be a better boss as a result.

As success comes, keep your feet on the ground. Take your promotions, advancements, and authority with a grain of salt. Take pains to show others how important they are to you and how much you count on them. If there are areas in which their ability obviously surpasses yours, don't hesitate to tell them about it. Be easy to live with.

Success is a wonderful thing—but a lot more wonderful if you share it. There are enough kinds of success in this world so everyone can have some. Make a point of recognizing the abilities of the people who work with you. They'll like you better—and cooperate better—if you do.

Quiet Self-Confidence

A successful boss, be he or she a supervisor or a company president, usually radiates quiet self-confidence. His attitude indicates he feels he has the authority and the ability to handle whatever comes up.

He doesn't flaunt his authority, because he doesn't feel any need to. He isn't trying to impress people, just doing his job. That enables him to give orders and instructions in a casual, non-offensive manner.

Furthermore, good bosses don't take it as a personal offense if someone doesn't do exactly what he's been told. They don't jump to the conclusion that anyone is defying their authority. They investigate first, to find out what's wrong.

Mostly, if you're the boss, people will do what you ask without argument. If they don't, the best assumption is, not that they are defying your authority, but they must have a pretty good reason. The first thing to do is to find out what it is. A self-confident boss does so without feeling the necessity for blowing his stack first, and perhaps looking ridiculous in the process.

Self-confident people stand criticism better too. It doesn't crush them. They examine it carefully, and, if the shoe fits, they put it on. They realize nobody is so perfect he can't learn. Criticism, and having people differ with you, is part of growing, part of groping toward the best solutions.

People who are reasonably sure of themselves criticize more tactfully too. They don't feel a need to take the person being criticized down a peg. They don't try to act superior when they criticize. They merely try to present a helpful point of view and make it as easy and unembarrassing as possible for the other person to consider.

People who are reasonably sure of themselves are not easily insulted, either. They know they are fairly capable even though considerably less than perfect. But they don't put themselves on a pedestal. They like themselves enough so they can take an insult with a grain of salt and perhaps even get some benefit out of it. People who criticize them in an effort to hurt them sometimes find they have accepted the criticism graciously and benefited from it instead.

When somebody loses control and makes some remarks he shouldn't, self-confident bosses don't take it as a personal offense. They don't even act disturbed. First they keep their cool. Then they try to find out what caused the upset. Finally, they get the person calmed down and settled down without making a big deal of it. They develop a talent for making molehills out of mountains, not mountains out of molehills.

How can you be a quietly self-confident boss if you're not really self-confident? Be an actor. Start pretending you're a quietly self-confident person and act that way.

We've tried to describe here how a self-confident, capable boss acts. Why not start acting that way yourself? If you obviously fail, sit down and think it over. Where did you go wrong? Resolve that next time you are going to do better. If you seriously resolve to handle the next situation better, you probably will. Improvement is not impossible, it's within the reach of every one of us. The important thing is to recognize where you've gone wrong and correct it. Don't just make the same kind of mistake over and over.

Ask yourself, again and again, how would a calmly self-confident person have handled this situation that I just messed up? What did I do wrong? How will I handle it the next time? Then do it. And don't worry about past mistakes. They are behind you. Just concentrate on doing better the next time. It may seem like an uphill road but just concentrate on the fact that you ARE making progress. That's what's important.

What Makes a Good Boss?

Have you ever worked for a good boss? In the first 15 years of my business life I rattled around a bit and had quite a few bosses, eight of them all told. Two were excellent, the rest ranged from so-so to rather poor.

How do you tell a good boss when you see one? Certain characteristics are common to all of them.

One is a pleasant disposition. They are never grim. They try to keep the work situation as pleasant as possible both for themselves and the people who work for them.

Second, no matter how much or how little you are paid, they don't take you for granted. They don't expect people to work for money alone. When you do a good job, they also express their personal appreciation.

They appreciate the difficulties of your job and the tough conditions you sometimes have to work under. And they show it. If you need help, they do their best to give it, or get it for you.

They appreciate the effort you make to do the job right. And mention to you the fact that they do notice it.

They appreciate your abilities—any unusual talents and background you bring to bear on your job. They don't treat you like a machine that is supposed to do these things anyway. When the job requires extra effort, talent, or dedication, they are the first to notice and thank you.

Yes, you are paid to do a good job. It's expected of you. But good bosses also add a personal touch. You know they appreciate your contributions because they never fail to notice them and tell you so.

Good bosses are enthusiastic and interested—in your work as well as their own. When you have a suggestion, they listen carefully and consider it fairly.

Think back to the bosses you personally were glad to stretch yourself for. How did they measure up in these respects? We suspect you'll find they measured up very well. And take a minute or two to think of the ones that didn't impress you. Where did they fall down on the job?

The point of this discussion is, of course, not them but you. How do you measure up in these areas? Do your attitude and actions occasionally leave something to be desired?

It's a serious mistake to rely on money alone to get the performance you want out of people. Yes, it will work with some people. It may also work with other people for a little while. But most people, day after day, year after year, need more than money to keep them interested in making their best efforts. They all like personal attention and appreciation. Some of them need it desperately. Fortunately, no matter how much of these extras you give, they'll always be interested in more.

Teamwork

Teamwork is no accident. It's not a matter of luck or chance. Bosses create teamwork—or kill it—by the way they treat people.

Employees begin to show teamwork when they feel they are a respected and valuable part of an operation. Making them feel that way is something a good boss works at.

Teamwork is a product of sharing—sharing interest, information, responsibilities, and credit. It's something that no strictly self-centered executive can hope to achieve. Bosses who are concerned primarily with advancing their own image and importance might as well forget about teamwork. They are not going to inspire any.

Teamwork starts with sharing information about what's going on in a department or in a company. How can people be expected to be members of a team if nobody cares enough about them and their efforts to keep them well-informed? How can they help achieve the department or company objectives if they haven't even been told what the objectives are and what they are supposed to accomplish?

Sharing responsibilities helps teamwork too. When people are given definite assignments, then relied on to carry them out, it builds their self-esteem. They are glad to be on a team where they amount to something. Bosses who hold all responsibilities close to their chests will never have a team. They really don't want one.

Does a boss act as if he or she were the kingpin, the only important factor in his operation? Cross him off the list. He won't develop teamwork that way. People enjoy teamwork because it makes them feel more important. They are a significant part of a meaningful effort.

Lastly, what about credit? Does the boss give credit generously and freely? Does he or she point out the importance of those who are helping him? The bosses who are the best at creating teamwork are the kind of people who think of themselves as members of a team, not as individual stars.

Maybe you've never thought much about team efforts, or why some people seem to achieve them, others don't. Think back a moment and you'll find that every important team effort has a strong background of sharing—interest, information, responsibilities, and credit. And that feeling comes from the top. It simply doesn't happen without those factors. People who think they've had good teamwork without these factors are usually kidding themselves.

When you achieve top-notch teamwork, everybody seems to know what's going on. They understand what the group is trying to achieve and why. Ideas flow freely. Sometimes, as a company grows from a small one to larger size, information doesn't get around as widely as it used to. Special efforts are required to see that everyone is kept informed. People can't be interested in something unless they are informed about it. And they can't feel like a team unless they have something in common to draw them together. Keeping those elements present is management's constant problem.

One new company president, who faced the problem of pulling together a company that was on the verge of bankruptcy, started inviting blue collar workers to have breakfast with him several days a week. The workers called it "Biscuits with Billy". He also invited the whole office to have a few beers every quarter the earnings went up. Silly? Not so you'd notice it. He had a bad situation and needed something unusual to pull people together. It worked like a charm. The morale problems have vanished; their other problems have been mastered too.

Have a Second Thought First

Most of the mistakes in handling people are made, not because the person who bungled didn't know better, but simply because he or she didn't stop to think. He didn't pause to appreciate the fact that the other person would have some feelings in the matter, and exactly what those feelings were likely to be.

It isn't just a problem of being impulsive, even though the impulsive action in any situation is often the wrong one. It's a matter of not stopping to realize that other people may have different points of view. The person who reacts impulsively in any situation is considering only one point of view—his or her own. But so are some people who don't act impulsively. Even though they take their time considering their own likes and dislikes, and their own advantages and disadvantages, they don't stretch their imaginations sufficiently to picture how others will feel.

The boss who wants to make good decisions has to have second thoughts. And the time to have them is before you make the decision, not after. Try to think of all the various people involved or affected by any decision you are asked to make. Does the decision you expect to make treat all of them equally? Are you setting a precedent? If you do this, will you also be obliged, later, to follow up by doing something else, something you really don't approve of? If you're not sure of your decision, sleep on it first.

When you are going to approach someone about a problem, and you hope to reach a certain decision, think it over carefully first. If you were in their shoes, how would you react? How is it likely to affect their pride, ambition, or pocketbook?

When you first bring up the subject, don't set out immediately to try to sell your own point of view. Show your consideration for their point of view, and show it immediately. Make it obvious that you have already been considering the other person's interests by the manner in which you bring up the subject. Admit there may be some good reasons for the way they feel. But then tell them why you hope they will consider another answer, one which you think might be more satisfactory. Think it over from their point of view and figure out the aspects that might appeal to them.

If you can't figure out what the other person's point of view might be, ask him or her first, before you try to sell yours. Find out what the situation is before you needlessly tread on anyone's feelings. Take time to consider their point of view, and show you appreciate why they feel that way. Then, without offending anyone, suggest the other point of view you hope they will also consider.

If there are obvious objections to your recommended solution, admit them quickly. Don't let people get all worked up pointing them out. Then, despite the objections, point out why you still think it is probably the best course of action. Please note that we said PROBABLY the best course of action. Anyone who claims to know what is DEFINITELY the best course of action is being offensively omniscient. No matter how sure you may be that the odds are in your favor, it rarely pays to be too positive.

Whenever you are tempted to open your mouth and sound off about something, put yourself in other people's shoes first. Imagine or find out what other people think before you say something antagonistic or offensive. Make thinking first a habit. It's a good sign of growing maturity.

Temper, Temper

If you have a hot temper, and have always had one, you may figure there's not much you can do about it. But if you're interested in moving up the executive ladder, we suggest you think it over a bit. Lots of people have learned to control their tempers. And a volatile temper is one of the most damaging management handicaps you can possibly have.

An easily aroused temper invariably hurts your results; it also lessens the respect people have for you—not only the people who work for you but the people above you as well.

The plain fact is that when you lose your temper—or let temper or resentment influence your thinking— you're not being smart. You're being stupid. And that's true no matter who you are and no matter at what level. When your temper is aroused, you are reacting with your glands, not your brain.

One of the most important management talents is the ability to refrain from getting angry, regardless of the provocation. Why get angry? An angry reaction is never a smart one. When you do something in anger, it's almost never the intelligent thing to do. You do it because it satisfies your irritation, not because it makes sense.

And what is it that makes most of us angry? Usually

it's when someone has shown lack of respect for us. The image we have of ourselves has been offended. So, conceited souls that we are, we get furious. Instead, we should simply be curious. Is our image that important to us? Is anyone else's opinion really worth getting angry about? How ridiculous!

The people who keep moving up in business are usually those who have learned to keep their tempers and other emotions well under control. Handling people skillfully demands self-control. People who want to be good at managing others must first learn to control themselves.

Experienced, capable bosses resist emotional impulses and temperamental decisions. When they feel temper rising, they break off what they are doing and get themselves in hand. They think about how foolish they have been acting, and resolve not to be a silly victim of their own emotions. When they resume discussing the situation, they do so with their personal feelings and prejudices firmly disciplined.

Smart bosses don't treat people vindictively. They don't—spitefully—give people the treatment they might obviously deserve. Instead, they keep their feelings and emotions out of it. They treat people in the manner which they—thinking cooly and logically —feel will be most effective.

It's easy to become angry with people—errors, mistakes, and even incompetence wear on your nerves.

They are hard to take. But the fact remains that the best way to get people to do better work is NOT to blow your stack. Being temperamental and losing your temper are not constructive. The best results come from having faith in people despite their faults, putting each day's failures behind you, and starting the next day with a positive, optimistic approach.

A positive approach starts with faith—even though it may at times seem a blind faith—that people can learn to do better work. Managers and supervisors who get people to do better work start by believing that they are capable of it. They keep appreciating people's good points—few as they may sometimes seem—and avoid emphasizing the bad. They keep stressing the reasons and rewards for doing good work, not the penalties for poor work.

Have you ever worked for someone who never lost his or her temper, who always had a cheerful positive approach? It's a pleasure—a pleasure you are in a position to give as well as receive.

Loyalty Pays

Loyalty is a special form of enduring friendship. If it's real, it sticks with you through thick and thin. It's a great feeling to know that the people you work for, and who work for you, are loyal. They aren't just going through the motions for the sake of making a buck. You know they also like you and will stand up for you if the occasion arises.

The best way to get loyalty is by giving it. Maybe the company you work for isn't perfect—no organization is. Perhaps your boss is less than perfect too. And, undoubtedly, the people who work for you leave something to be desired.

Nevertheless, if you're loyal, instead of concentrating on their defects, you try to appreciate their good points. You stick up for them and encourage them to do their best. You don't talk them down behind their backs, and when the chips are down, they can count on you.

This is the standard we should all try to live by no matter where we work or who works for us. Why? Because it gets better results and it's good for us. It's a fact of business life that organizations where people like each other, and are loyal to each other, work better. You appreciate loyalty in others and they appreciate it in you.

Unfortunately, a great many people like to be critical of the places where they work and the people they work with. Many of them are personally very capable. But they lessen their value as members of a team by constantly running down other members instead of lifting them up.

There's only one attitude worth having wherever you work. That's a positive attitude, an encouraging one, that concentrates on helping to make things better. People who make a career of idle criticism are wasting their time, no matter how justified it may be.

Whether you're happy or disgruntled with the people you work with depends, to a great extent, on which side of the coin you look at. If you look at the bad side, you can find fault with almost any setup. But there is also a good side in every situation. Be sure you take a look at that.

There's another angle too. As long as you are going to work for an organization, how can you be half-hearted about it and still do a good job? When the people who work for you sense your negative attitude toward the company, how can you expect theirs to be any better? And if they sense that you really don't give a hoot about them, personally, how can they care about you?

This doesn't mean you must never criticize. But there's a time and place for constructive criticism. The time is when you are alone with whomever is involved. The place is in private. And the manner is strictly friendly, not unfriendly, obviously soft-pedaled to spare the person's feelings, and obviously made not to hurt but possibly to help.

That's legitimate criticism—the kind made by a loyal friend or boss—hopefully to improve the situation. Criticism that can't accomplish anything, that simply makes people angry, is a horse of a different color.

Loyalty pays—loyalty to everyone. If you don't make room for it in your world, that world will be a shrinking, dingy place. People have maneuvered to become company presidents, occasionally, without being loyal to anyone but themselves. But a successful foreman with a dozen loyal, appreciative employees gets more out of life than they do.

Explain Why

Bosses, theoretically, are supposed to tell people what to do. Actually, it's far better to ask people to do something—and it doesn't hurt to say please. Then explain why you want them to do it.

A good boss doesn't just order people to do things. He or she doesn't treat people like robots. He explains what he would like them to do and why, so they can see that it makes sense and question it if they don't understand. He treats them like thinking people, not puppets. He never acts like a superior being giving instructions about something he alone can understand.

Explaining the reasons why always makes "orders" easier to take. It shows that nobody is pushing anybody around. It's obviously something that needs to be done and somebody has to do it.

Explaining your requests makes your orders easier to follow. There's much less chance that someone will do something that doesn't make sense. He or she will have a much better chance of knowing why it does or doesn't make sense if you explain it first.

Explaining the reasons for various requests makes people feel more important. If they know why they are asked to do something, they feel more in on things. It enables them to use their brains as well as their hands and their backs.

For example, why give a man a shipment order and simply tell him to get it out in a hurry? Why not tell him: "This is for X Company. We've guaranteed they can have it today. If we miss, we may lose their next order. Get it moving. If you hit any problems, let me know."

If you have rules people must observe, take some time to explain them. Be sure everybody knows why you have the rules. What would be the possible harm if you didn't have the rules? A little explanation will show why most rules are necessary. If they can't be justified, they shouldn't exist.

Tell people the reasons for everything they are interested in. A business shouldn't have arbitrary rules or customs. It shouldn't have rules just for the sake of annoying people. Anything that can't be explained in a way that makes sense should be changed until it does.

Make it a habit NOT to tell people what to do and stop there. Also tell them why. Correct, prompt information cuts mistakes, rumors, and harmful speculation. If you don't know why you are asking people to do something, find out. Orders and rules that people don't understand are annoying.

Unfortunately, there are many employees who have

to do things day after day that they do not fully understand the reasons for. And how can they be interested or enthusiastic, or have helpful suggestions, about something they don't understand? It makes people with any brains feel like cogs in a machine.

The people who work for you are supposed to do what you tell them to do. But they'll feel a lot better about it if, instead of issuing orders, you simply ask them to do it and explain why. They'll also do it with greater understanding. Why be a big, pompous order-giver when you don't have to be? There are too many of them in this world already.

Authority—a Necessary Evil

Most people like jobs that have titles, the loftier sounding the better. A title helps show what their authority is. It is more impressive to their friends and associates than a job with no title.

A certain amount of authority, which usually accompanies a title, is important in most jobs. Somebody has to have the final say. Somebody has to have the final responsibility. But other than that, titles are mostly a matter of catering to an individual's self-image.

On their own, titles don't accomplish much. They may convey a certain amount of authority, but that's no guarantee the power will be used ably or intelligently. They may impress outsiders at first, but the effect will rub off very quickly if performance doesn't match the picture conveyed by the job title.

Authority and fancy titles can be heady stuff, especially if a person isn't used to them. Many people have a tendency to take them too seriously, to let them go to their heads. In the long run, however, regardless of title, you are what you are, and you do what you can do. Titles don't change that a bit. That's why capable people don't try to hide behind titles, or even pay much attention to them. They concentrate on the fact that they have a job to do and go ahead and do it.

An unfortunate thing is that the more important some people feel, often because of their impressive titles, the more they forget or ignore the principles of leadership. If people jump when they speak, why bother to explain and persuade? Using their authority, and simply telling the lesser beings in this world what to do, seems like the easiest way to get things done. And what difference do the feelings of these lower echelon people make anyway?

Actually, they make a tremendous difference. The difference between good morale and poor morale, between teamwork and no teamwork, between good productivity and poor productivity.

Authority of some sort is necessary in most jobs. But it's never an adequate substitute for leadership. The principles and practices of good human relations and good psychology apply to the top jobs in a company just as much as they do to the jobs of foreman or supervisor. People who are good at inspiring others and developing a spirit of teamwork always outperform bosses who simply depend on their authority. No matter how great anyone's authority may be, the best it can generate is compliance. It will never make people stretch themselves wholeheartedly. The authoritative approach never creates goodwill.

The real power of any boss lies, not in his or her authority, but in the ability to keep people interested in doing a good job. A boss who starts to rely on authority, has fallen down on the job of leadership.

To make this world work—at least with the mass production of our current society—we have to have bosses. In a way, that's unfortunate. Nobody really likes to be bossed. The best we can hope for is that people who move into positions of authority will keep their heads and use it as lightly and sparingly as possible.

When problems arise, do you keep your patience and try to interest people in doing the job right? Do you try to find out what's keeping people from doing a better job? Do you make a real effort to get cooperation? Or do you just start pushing people around?

Save your authority for emergency use only. Don't let it blind you to the need for leadership.

How to Disagree Tactfully

People disagree about a lot of things. As long as it's something on which they don't have to agree, and nobody gets unpleasant about it, it doesn't make much difference. It's no skin off anybody's nose.

But there are situations where you and your associates, in order to be effective, have to agree on a course of action. Perhaps you, as the boss, have the final say. But you hope that as many of your associates as possible will share your point of view. You also want the others to at least understand why you think it's the right choice. The last thing you want is personal resentment of your decision. You need their cooperation in making it work.

So—take it easy. Make haste slowly. Whenever a subject comes up on which there might be considerable disagreement, don't start the discussion with bold statements one way or the other. Just talk a while and see what points of view come out. Wait until you can see what the differences are. Then you can express your own point of view in a manner that will be least offensive and most effective.

Just remember this: No matter how much authority you have, you can't FORCE other people to think you are right. If you want their wholehearted cooperation—not just compliance—you have to work for it. Furthermore, people aren't going to believe you're right solely because of logic. They may do what you say, but they won't believe you're right unless they WANT to believe you're right.

When it's obvious that, in some respects at least, your opposition is dead wrong, there's always a temptation to say so in no uncertain terms. But it's not the smart thing to do—why take a chance of hurting someone's pride unnecessarily? It's more effective— especially since you want their cooperation—to disagree reluctantly and hesitantly. Make it obvious that you don't like to disagree with the other person but you feel it's necessary to at least consider another point of view.

Before you disagree with people, be sure you understand what their arguments are and why. Repeat them to show that you understand, and admit that there are good reasons for feeling that way. But then go further —explain your own reasons why you can't convince yourself that their answer is the best course of action.

One of the most tactful and inoffensive methods of disagreeing with other people is by trying to agree with them. Encourage them to explain their views while you listen and ask questions in a sympathetic effort to understand and agree with their point of view. Finally, point out reluctantly why you still can't agree, and see if they have any further information that might change your point of view.

Basically, there is no reason why people should be offended when you disagree with them, as long as you do it in a tactful and open-minded manner. So watch yourself. When topics are up for discussion, when people obviously have different opinions, take it easy. You want the cooperation and help of people who may not agree 100% with the course of action decided on as well as those who approve. Don't make enemies unnecessarily.

Show Respect

Handling people successfully, day after day, is not a matter of cleverness. Cleverness might work once or twice, but after that people will get wise to you. You can't fool everybody all the time.

In dealing with the people who work for you the only tactics worth considering are those that are honest, sound, and consistent. People soon know you for exactly what you are—selfish, unselfish, fair or unfair. It's a waste of time to try to trick them.

If people like you as a boss, they'll work harder and better for you than for someone they don't like. And if you want people to like you, it's important to sho﹅ that you respect them, their individuality, their rights, and their feelings. You can't treat them like so many bodies that occasionally come in handy.

Human beings are pretty independent creatures—or they would like to be—regardless of their status. Very few of us enjoy having bosses. We submit to authority because we have to, not because we like it. And most of us think we are just as good as the people who boss us around.

That's why, when the boss shows a healthy respect for us, and treats us like people who really matter, we appreciate it. It helps to ease our resentment at following his or her orders, and makes a job more pleasant and satisfying. On the other hand, if you know the boss doesn't respect you, there's always something lacking.

But what if you don't respect the kind of people who work for you, and there's nothing you can do about it? First let's be sure you're not confusing respect with admiration. If you don't admire some people who work for you, that's understandable. You can't force yourself to admire someone.

But respecting people is a different matter. You can still respect people whether you admire them and like them, or not. You can respect their rights and their feelings. You can show you feel they have just as much right to be on this planet as you have. By doing so you can show that you are a decent human being, a good person to work for, not just a self-centered s.o.b. trying to exploit everyone else for your own benefit.

Respect for the rights and importance of every individual is part and parcel of being an effective leader. All employees, from clerk to president, have a right to pride, hopes, ambitions, and feelings. Nobody, in the eyes of God, is any more important than anyone else. The boss who shows a healthy appreciation of this fact is always better to work for, and, other things being equal, will always get better results.

What do you want most from your boss? Think it over and you'll find respect comes right at the top of the list. Why should the people who work for you be any different?

There are many ways to show respect. By ordinary politeness. By asking people's opinions. By carrying your authority lightly and using it only when necessary to get a job done, not flaunting it and acting as though you were a V.I.P. A good boss creates an atmosphere of mutual respect and teamwork, not an aura of superiority or condescension.

Criticize Intelligently

Whenever you are tempted to criticize anyone, stop. Does it really make sense? If so, what is the best way to do it?

The purpose of criticism is NOT to punish people. An organization that depends on punishment to make people do what they ought to do is in a bad way. Punishment is an ineffective, counterproductive tool. No intelligent, experienced manager would think of using it, except as a last resort. And probably not then.

The purpose of criticism is NOT to express your personal resentment. Expressing resentment is not a constructive way to influence people.

The only legitimate purpose of criticism is to help the recipient do better work in the future. If what you have in mind isn't likely to do that, show masterful self-control and forget it. Don't approach a person whose attitude or work has been unsatisfactory until you think you have figured out a way to make him or her WANT to do better. Voluntarily. Wholeheartedly, if possible.

Until you've figured out an approach that has a chance of striking the person in a favorable manner, don't waste your breath. True, he or she might deserve a tongue-lashing. But what good will it actually do?

Don't waste your effort on fruitless, spiteful, comments. Think! What might inspire this person to improve? There must be some better approach than simply irritating him or her and making him resentful.

The most effective way to criticize is almost always in a friendly, casual manner. Don't give the person the idea that you are rushing into a situation and are anxious to start tearing him or her apart. Take your time. Be curious. Ask questions about whatever the trouble is. Find out the person's version of how it happened. See how he or she thinks it could be corrected, or at least improved. Without anger, point out matter-of-factly, in simple language, how this situation hurts the company and why it ought to be corrected. Then find out what the person would suggest to improve the situation.

If people you are criticizing agree that something has been wrong, and come up with a good suggestion for changing it, congratulate them. Tell them you'll be glad to try their solution. Can you count on them to help make it work?

If they don't have any idea of how to correct the situation, suggest what you think they ought to do. See what they think of that. Is there anything they object to? Is there anything else they think would work better? Point out that nobody is trying to punish them personally. You're just looking for a solution that will work better and that they will cooperate in.

With this kind of approach, you'll find that many people will willingly—or reluctantly—admit their responsibility and agree to help improve the situation. They are more apt to recognize at least partial responsibility than they would be if you angrily attacked them.

Can you think of anything which the person or persons involved do well, not poorly? While you're seeking their cooperation in this problem, it never hurts to point out how well they have performed or cooperated in other respects. They will appreciate it.

No matter how seriously you question people's actions, never question their motives. Who knows what someone's motives are? How can you prove it? If you know for a fact that someone has bad motives, it would be wise to find a way to get rid of that person as soon as possible. As long as you keep someone with you, however, always credit him or her with good motives. Assume they are trying to do what is right and good for the company.

Remember the old saying, "Give a dog a good name and he'll try to live up to it." That's sound psychology. If you show that you firmly believe people want to do better work, it encourages them to believe it too. You give them a favorable picture of themselves, and inspire them to live up to it.